Lahore

Lahore

Mohamed Amin · Duncan Willetts
Brendan Farrow

Ferozsons (Pvt.) Ltd.

LAHORE–RAWALPINDI–KARACHI

ACKNOWLEDGEMENTS

The Publishers wish to thank especially the Director of Lahore Museum, Dr. Saifur Rahman Dar, for the historical research upon which this book is based and for preparing an original manuscript for our reference; also Mr Liaquot Gill of the Pakistan Government Tourism Ministry for invaluable guidance and assistance around the city; Mr A. Rahman, Editor of Viewpoint Magazine, for an illuminating interview; Mr Zaheer Salam and Ferozsons (Pvt) Ltd, Lahore; the Pakistan Tourism Development Corporation; and Pakistan International Airlines.

First published 1988 by
Ferozsons (Pvt) Ltd.,
60, Shahrah-e-Quaid-e-Azam,
Lahore, Pakistan

ISBN 969-0-00694-0

© 1988 by Camerapix

This book was designed and produced by
Camerapix Publishers International,
P.O. Box 45048,
Nairobi, Kenya.

Consultant: Dr Saifur Rahman Dar, Director Lahore Museum
Editor: Brian Tetley
Design: Craig Dodd
Typeset: Nazma Rawji

Printed in Hong Kong by
Mandarin Offset

Contents

1 Pearl of the Punjab

"I have purchased Lahore with my life.
By giving my life for Lahore,
Actually I have purchased another Paradise." — Empress Nur Jahan.

A shell haphazardly exploding during the 1545 siege of Kalinjar in northern India brought an untimely but perhaps fortunate end to the reign of the gifted upstart King, Sher Shah Suri. He had reigned only five years, but in that time had shown himself worthy of a place in the splendid line of early Mughal Emperors of South Asia into which he, a usurper had intruded. Like the early Mughals themselves this "Lion King", Sher Shah, distinguished himself as a builder – though little of what he built remains today apart from some roads: notably the Great Trunk still running all the way across the north of the Indian subcontinent and linking Kabul with Calcutta. As he built it this formidable highway made the arduous journey a realistic undertaking even in the hottest and driest of Indian weather; for it was equipped with rest-places (serais) every 15 kilometres where relay messengers could change horses, and merchants and other travellers could take rest and refreshment – especially clean well-water – all the way to their destination. Yet, unlike the Mughals, this creative ruler built virtually nothing in the great city of Lahore. Deliberately.

It was not that he despised the Pearl of the Punjab; on the contrary he saw it through the eyes of the covetous would-be ruler he had been. "Such a large city should not exist on the very road of an invader," he had often brooded. "Once he has taken Lahore he has all he needs to resupply his forces." As Sher Shah Suri lay dying of the injuries he took from that shell-burst, he voiced a savage regret: that he had not destroyed Lahore.

The world can be thankful.

Yet for all its quirkiness, this soldier king's remorse reflected the essence of Lahore's fatal individuality: its twin characteristics of wealth and vulnerability. Each was linked directly to the city's geographical situation.

Centrally placed in the vast, and lush, ancient triangular plain of the Punjab, Lahore was a natural market place not only in the region but, especially as encouraged and developed by the early Mughals and Sher Shah Suri, also for the great cities of Central Asia to the northwest and as far to the northeast as China.

At the same time it was the natural midway staging place for Afghan armies marching to plunder the fabled riches of Delhi. With no natural defences other than the unpredictable river Ravi, Lahore was easy meat to both them and the countless other fierce warrior hordes forever sweeping down from the Hindu Kush and Himalaya foothills to take their fill from the rich, but vulnerable table set before them.

Lahore was well named Pearl of Punjab; but she was ever a pearl fatally easy to plunder.

Opposite: Lively folk dance celebrates Pakistan's most famous festival, the National Horse and Cattle Show staged each year at Lahore's spacious Fortress Stadium. The finest livestock in the country, arena events with dancing animals, tent-pegging, and other contests, music and military tattoos, are all featured.

Title Page: Minar-e-Pakistan in Iqbal Park commemorates Muslim League's historic resolution calling for creation of Pakistan in March 1940. Contents Page: Sundown's glow frames famed Badshahi Mosque, most celebrated of all Lahore's architectural splendours.

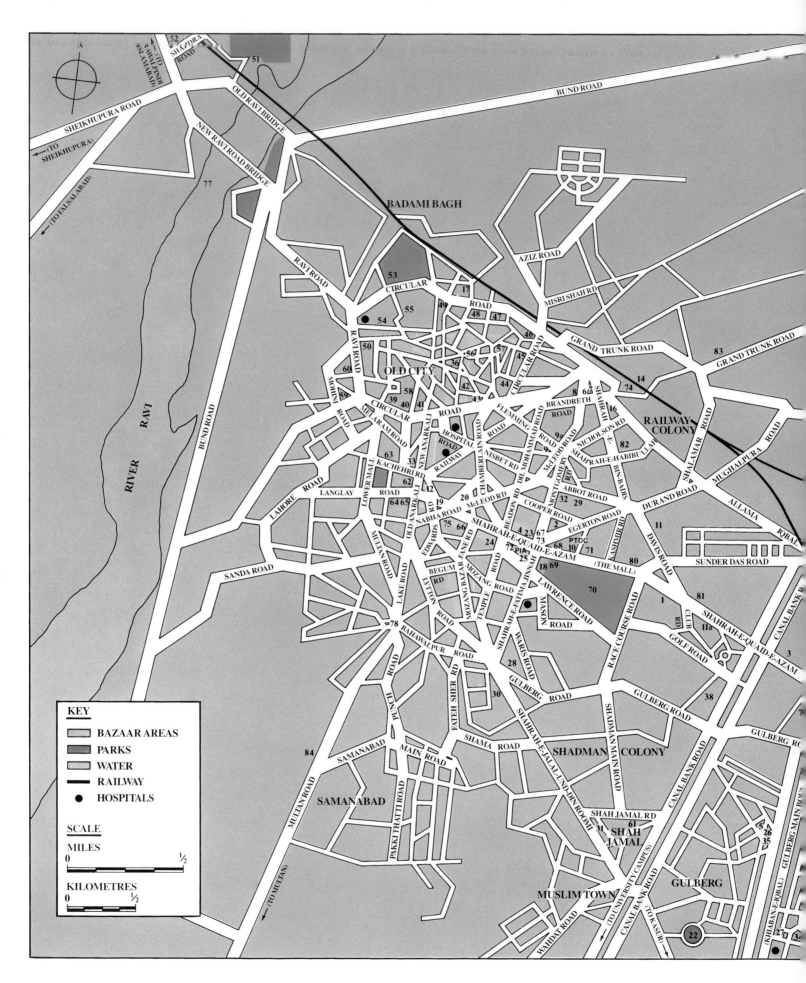

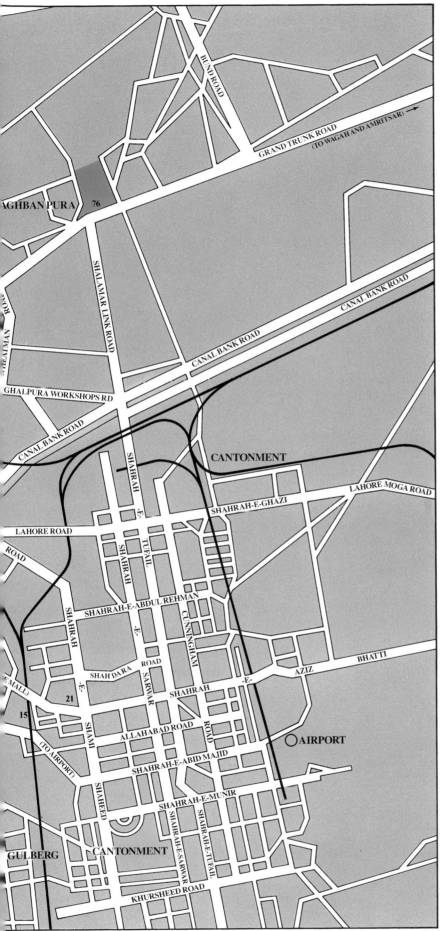

Hotels

1. Lahore Pearl Continental, Shahrah-e-Quaid-e-Azam
2. Faletti's Hotel, Egerton Road
3. International Hotel, Shahrah-e-Quaid-e-Azam
4. Indus Hotel, Shahrah-e-Quaid-e-Azam
5. Zonobi's Hotel, Main Market Gulberg
6. Hotel Asia, near City Railway Station
7. Parkway Hotel, near City Railway Station
8. Braganza Hotel, near Railway Station
9. Orient Hotel, McLeod Road
9a. Lahore Hotel, McLeod Road
10. Lahore Hilton, Shahrah-e-Quaid-e-Azam
11. Ambassador Hotel, Davis Road
11a. Motel Country Club, Shahrah-e-Quaid-e-Azam

Hostels

12. Y.M.C.A. Shahrah-e-Quaid-e-Azam
13. Youth Hostel, 110-B Firdous Market, Gulberg III

Railway Stations

14. Lahore City Station
15. Lahore Cantonment Station

Bus Stations

16. G.T.S. main Bus Station
17. General Bus Stand, Badami Bagh

Police Stations

18. Civil Lines, Tel: 67458/68890

Post & Telegraph Offices

19. General Post Office, Shahrah-e-Quaid-e-Azam
20. Telegraph Office, Shahrah-e-Quaid-e-Azam

Stadiums

21. Fortress Stadium, Lahore Cantt.
22. Gaddafi Stadium

Cinema Houses

23. Al-Falah Cinema
24. Victory Cinema
25. Plaza Cinema
26. Auriga Cinema
27. Capri Cinema
28. Angola Cinema
29. Mubarik Cinema
30. Sanam Cinema
31. Galaxy Cinema
32. Gulistan Cinema

Shopping Areas

33. Anarkali Bazaar (Bano Bazaar) Shahrah-e-Quaid-e-Azam
34. Liberty Market
35. Gulberg Main Market
36. Shah Alam Market: (Kashmiri Bazaar, Suha Bazaar, Dabbi Bazaar, Chatta Bazaar)

Clubs

37. Lahore Gymkhana
38. Punjab Club

Gates

39. Bhati Gate
40. Mori Gate
41. Lahori Gate
42. Shah Alami Gate
43. Mochi Gate
44. Akbari Gate
45. Delhi Gate
46. Yakki Gate
47. Sheranwala Gate
48. Kashmiri Gate
49. Masti Gate
50. Texali Gate

Places of Interest

51. Jehangir's Tomb
52. Nur Jehan's Tomb
53. Minar-e-Pakistan
54. Badshahi Mosque & Allama Iqbal's Tomb
55. Lahore Fort
56. Golden Mosque
57. Wazir Khan's Mosque
58. Faqir Khana (Museum)
59. Shrine of Data Ganj Bakhsh
60. Shrine of Pir Makki
61. Shrine of Shah Jamal
62. Punjab University (old campus)
63. Gov. College, Lahore
64. Zamzama (Kim's Gun)
65. Museum
66. Punjab High Court
67. Provincial Assembly Hall
68. Wapda House
69. Zoological Gardens
70. Bagh-e-Jinnah
71. Arts Council
72. Masjid-e-Shuhada
73. Summit Minaret
74. Dai Anga's Mosque
75. State Bank of Pakistan
76. Shalamar Garden
77. River Ravi
78. Chauburji
79. Golf Course
80. Governor's House
81. Aitchison College
82. Railway Head Quarters
83. Engineering University

Tourist Transport

37. Gymkhana Tours
2. Din-Tours, Hotel Faletti's
1. Din-Tours, Pearl Continental
84. Automobile Association PTDC, Transport House, Egerton Road

Above: Mughal leaders had a passion for the chase and hunting. They rode on caparisoned elephants with beaters and attendants at the alert, as this painting of the Mughal era in Lahore Museum illustrates.

The practical recourse, obviously, was to fortify. For as long as records tell of Lahore, they recount the many buildings, rebuildings, modifications and enlargements of its citadel fortress. Until the Mughals, however, it was of earth – inadequate against the ferocity and determination of those with little to lose and everything to gain from successful conquest. Besides, the Fort could only ever be a bastion, the bulwark of the city's defence – nothing like adequate to contain the relatively huge population attracted to Lahore by its early prosperity. Before the end of the 16th century the total population was around half a million: for the age, a huge number: and in fact the same as when, four centuries later, Lahore was named Western Province capital at the time Pakistan achieved Independence.

Lahore had been great long before the Mughals. There was a first Golden Age under the Ghaznivide rulers – inadequately documented, true, but still with plenty of evidence of the status of the city as one of the Muslim world's chief cultural centres. Indeed, Lahore's history at this time (1059-1186) reads like a prelude to the Mughal glory to come. Not only was it favoured in its rulers, but also in the intellectuals, poets, saints and artists who flocked to the city: though today only four tombs and some coins bear any witness.

From the end of the 12th century, however, through most of the next three centuries till Babur came, Lahore's lot was unhappy, and all the time subordinate. It was the Mughals who founded for good and ever the glory and renown of the Punjab's "Pearl City": bringing to it not only the greatest quantity of the superb architecture named for them anywhere in their domains, but also a train of spiritual, intellectual, cultural life without compare in the sub-continent.

It was the greatest of the Mughal rulers, Akbar – his name means the Great – who gave the city its first solid, brick-built fortress. It stands still. But even that mighty structure, like any castle in Europe, was essentially for the local ruler to live in, with his troops, and for the local citizens to repair to – as best they could, and only as many as could be accommodated – in time of attack. A city rich as Lahore became was in a sense doomed to submit, outside the walls of its riverside fortress, to constant devastation. It's important for today's visitor to bear that in mind.

Sadly it was not only external forces which savaged Lahore in attack. Forces within, under different titles, added their ravages. Just as Renaissance and later Popes tore down major architectural achievements of the ancient Romans such as the Colosseum, in order to build their own palaces, churches and monuments out of the ancient stones, so Sikh rulers of Lahore in the first half of the 19th century quarried the magnificent mausolea, pavilions and palaces of the Mughals for their own extrovert and opulently decorated temples and houses, strikingly different in spirit from the sometimes almost severe splendour of Muslim tradition.

Like the British, who succeeded them in power halfway through the century, the Sikhs also failed lamentably to respect what, to a Muslim people, was the sacred nature of many of the Mughal buildings. Both Sikhs and British abused the great Badshahi Mosque, for example – though after 50 years of control the British under Lord Curzon recognised they had behaved like iconoclasts and tried, often successfully, to make good the damage done.

Above: Citadel gateway marks Emperor Aurangzeb's only contribution to the fortress. It takes its name, Alamgiri, from one of his titles, meaning Conqueror of the World. The design – despite the lotus-leaf decoration – reflects the soldier king's uncompromising character. Of him, one enemy said: 'To fight Aurangzeb is to combat one's own destiny.'

Opposite: Ornate 17th century dome of Lahore's Wazir Khan mosque, named after the Punjab Viceroy of the Architect King, Shah Jahan.

Below: Glowing detail of the floral motifs and calligraphy, composed out of enamelled faience tiles, which adorn the interior of the Wazir Khan Mosque, built in 1663 during the reign of Shah Jahan.

Above: Faithful pray in the Hazarat Data Ganj Bakhsh Mosque. Islam came to the sub-continent by Mohamed bin Qasim's conquest of the Sind in AD 711, not long after the Prophet Muhammad's death.

Right: Lahore Museum's 15th century Qu'ran, printed in Afghanistan in AD 1442.

Professor Saifur Rahman Dar – Director of Lahore Museum, noted conservationist and an expert on the history of the region – is hard put to decide at whose hands the city suffered more: Sikh or British; though in their longer period of control the British at least established an Archaeological Department of Government, which succeeded in saving for posterity a number of Mughal monuments which would otherwise have been lost.

This fascinating and richly endowed city thus paid heavily for its wealth, beauty and vulnerability, and unhappily ranks as one of the most attacked, ransacked, pillaged, and virtually destroyed cities in civilisation's history.

Both splendour and spoliation are visible today. Here the emphasis is on the splendour: in the breathtaking brilliance of decor in the Wazir Khan mosque, for example, and the Shish Mahal; in the classic elegance and proportion in Shah Jahan's Shalamar Gardens, his Fort Quadrangle, and the dignified simplicity of the Moti Masjid (Pearl Mosque), and in the majesty of Aurangzeb's Badshahi Mosque. There you will regret the despoliation of the Asaf Khan and Ali Mardan Khan mausolea, of the Gateway to the Gulabi Bagh and the nearby Sarvwala Maqbara, and possibly more, the condition of the Fort's obviously once magnificent glazed wall and the Shah Burj that tops it.

The visitor must see the two together. It's the only way to know both what this city has been, and what this city has been through. Only then can Lahore's astonishing vitality be appreciated and rightly admired.

Above: Modern mosque, framed by the rays of the setting sun, marks the shrine of the mystic, Hazarat Data Ganj Bakhsh – Bestower of Favours – the Patron Saint of Lahore. Arriving in the city from Afghanistan in AD 1039, he stayed till his death thirty-three years later. He was buried near the mosque which he had built but which was later destroyed and replaced by the present one.

2 Promise and Travail

"One who hasn't seen Lahore," goes the ancient Punjabi adage, "hasn't been born!"

Extravagant language, maybe, but admirers have always vied with each other to immortalise this "Pearl of the Punjab" – itself the most coveted province of old Hindustan. Lahore is "Queen of cities"; others are "like a golden ring, she the diamond." In the 12th century a poet imprisoned in Persia yearned for Lahore as for a woman: "I want, some velvet from which emanates the fragrance of Lahore…For longing for Lahore heart and soul faint within me…" Through the centuries too, rapacious outsiders have violently underscored what the poets said. In blood.

The Punjab has always tempted invaders. Five rivers tumbling down off the world's Himalayan roof flow through this vast triangular plain, four to pay their separate tributes to the Indus before that legendary waterway issues into the Arabian Sea. They give the region its name – Punjab means Five Waters – and ensure the proverbial, and much-prized, fertility.

With rare exceptions invaders approached via one of the northwest passages from Afghanistan and the Hindu Kush; the way of Babur, founder of the Mughal Empire, and his ancestors Tamurlane and Genghis Khan – as well as of the earlier Greeks, Guptas, Mongols, Turks, Pathans, and the Aryans.

How many of them before the sixth century knew anything of Lahore is just not known. It cannot be said for certain that there was a Lahore more than 14 centuries ago; though strong tradition claims a birth date centuries earlier.

Legends in fact abound. Connection with the known invasion of the Indus Valley by Alexander the Great figures in several. Alexandria Bucephalos, for example, founded by the Greek military genius in 324 B.C. to commemorate his famous horse, has been identified with today's Lahore; a variant attributes the city's foundation to slaves left behind by Alexander when he turned for home.

The sixth century is the earliest date science can give. In May 1959 archaeological 'digs' under a very few parts of the old city revealed shards of pottery and various implements which went back that far; but nothing earlier. It is confidently predicted, however, that excavation on a more comprehensive scale would take the city's foundation back to at least the first century of the Christian era. Professor Dar supports this view, and bases his estimate on arguments that include local genealogical tables and the reference by the great Greek explorer-scientist Ptolemy (who flourished in 150 A.D) to the settlement of "Labokla" – which seems to have been one of Lahore's early names. In this theory the year 145 A.D. is proposed as the city's birth date, but Dr. Dar believes if Lahore existed then it was only as a small and insignificant village or town.

Opposite: Soaring minaret of modern Lahore in busy downtown district overlooks the 16th century Lahori Gate built by Akbar the Great.

Above: Typical of Lahore's ancient origins, this wooden balcony reflects an extrovert grandeur now overshadowed by modern high-rises.

Opposite: Fearful for the safety of one of the few remaining links with 11th century Lahore, a city philanthropist funded work for this concrete canopy over the tomb of Ayyaz, Governor of Lahore, during the rule of Mahmud of Ghazni. It was the Ghaznevide dynasty – AD 1021-1186 – which ended centuries of Hindu Rajput domination of Lahore and the Punjab.

One of the major headaches for anyone trying to trace Lahore's pedigree is the almost unbelievable number and variety of its names. At various times it has been called Parichhitpur, Samand Pal Nagari, Udinagar and Loharpur. Not until nearly 1000 A.D. did it begin to be consistently called anything like Lahore, and of that name it rejoiced in no fewer than 20 variations, from El Ahwar to Lahanur and Loharkotta. (With thinly disguised dismay Professor Dar notes that in the 12th century a scholar resident in the city used no fewer than five different versions of the name!) Add to this confusion Professor Dar's statement that "perhaps in the whole of South Asia there is no other place name which is claimed by so many cities and towns and even villages" and you begin to sympathise with the Pakistan Tourism Development Corporation writer who says simply: "The origins of Lahore are obscure and its history really began in 1021..."

Tempting as it is to leave it at that, mention of another significant conquerer, and one more fact about Lahore, must be made.

Islam came here in its earliest years. The bearer's name, appropriately, was Mohamed bin Qusim: a brilliant young general from Basra who marched a six thousand strong army into the Punjab by the hazardous coastal desert route from Persia, establishing his base short of Lahore – at Multan. Young Mohamed seems to have been too successful for his own good. He was early recalled to Basra and executed. Yet it was he who first brought Islam to the Punjab: a momentous event with profound implications for the whole subcontinent ever since.

The one more fact is complementary. While the city's recorded history

18

really begins in 1021 with the arrival of another Muslim conqueror, Mahmud of Ghazni, the Lahore which he conquered was Hindu – in fact the last stronghold in the region of the Hindu Shahi kingdom. The city's name in Hindu tradition means Fort of Loh – the son of Rama, hero of the 300 B.C. Sanskrit epic the *Ramayana*. Lahore Fort still shows a temple of Loh, near the Alamgiri gate. The river Ravi which then skirted the northern side was likewise named for one of the titles of the Hindu goddess Durga. Some also claim that the old city's Bhatti Gate takes its name from Rajput families who migrated to Rajisthan in 145 A.D.

The royal city of those Hindu Shahis was Kabul; but for more than 20 years their power in the Punjab had been contested with increasing determination by the Ghazni-based Afghan kingdom of Sabuktigin and his redoubtable warrior son Mahmud.

From his very childhood, chronicles say, this Mahmud "was bent on extirpating idolatry and establishing the religion of the Prophet on the land across the Indus". In September of the year 1000 he launched the first of many attacks on this northwestern corner of the subcontinent and in November 1001 inflicted such a humiliating defeat on his veteran Hindu enemy Jayapal that the Punjab ruler later killed himself – setting fire to his own bier.

Jayapal's son, Anandpal, fared little better; though in 1008, pressed by priests to drive the invaders out of the Indus Valley, he came close. Entering into a confederation with the Hindu rajas of India he engaged Mahmud's forces in a great battle near Peshawar. The Hindus fought with great courage and resolve. Records say that one furious charge of Ghakkars alone killed between three and four-thousand Muslim soldiers. Mahmud's men were on the point of being routed.

"But the tide of war suddenly turned," says the record. Anandpal was in the thick of the fray, pushing his advantage when, terrified by the fire-balls and arrows hurtling in all directions, his elephant abruptly fled, carrying the helpless commander off the battlefield. Believing they had been deserted by their leader the Hindu troops turned and ran: closely pursued by the astonished Muslims "who put great numbers to the sword".

Anandpal's son Trilochanpal was then assassinated by his own men.

So through a series of mighty battles – in which horsemen alone on the Hindu side might total 100,000 quite apart from the far greater "prodigious" number of foot soldiers – Mahmud established dominion over Lahore and the surrounding country so securely that, despite long continuing Hindu opposition, he achieved his lifelong ambition. For centuries, almost without interruption, the destiny of the Punjab as Muslim was assured, and Mahmud, consequently, is considered founder of the Muslim Empire upon the sub-continent.

Lahore now entered upon 150 years of physical, commercial, cultural and military development. Enlarged, it became the official capital of the province and, for several years, capital of the Empire. Its fortifications were strengthened; the fort itself rebuilt. Mahmud ordered the expansion – he had a mosque built on the site of an old temple to the sun and another incorporated in the fort – but much of the work is attributed to Malik Ayyaz, an army general whom Mahmud's successor, Masud, appointed to be regional governor and guardian of Majdud, the 18-year-old heir to the throne. Ayyaz must have been highly regarded to have been entrusted with such responsibility and it's a measure of the importance already attached to Lahore that this city was chosen as training ground for the ruler-to-be.

Masud succeeded the legendary Mahmud around 1030 and gave Ayyaz this

Below: Coins from the first half of the 11th century minted during the reign of Mahmud of Ghazni and now in Lahore Museum. Where they were minted remains a mystery.

appointment some time before 1040; though, as with all dates and names of the period, traditions vary and the continuity of names especially is often unsure. Who precisely should get credit for what is also often open to question. The chroniclers of the day in South Asia, as in Europe at the same time, generally cared less than modern historians for known facts, and rather more – perhaps like some modern journalists – with impressing their audience.

In 1042 both Ayyaz and his charge were found dead in their beds within a few days of each other and in similar circumstances: "of cause unknown". It should be said however that at the time of his death the young man's brother Maudud was also claiming the throne: and that would-be kings in southern Asia in the eleventh century were no more distinguished than their European contemporaries for observing the "niceties" of legal succession…

The middle decades of this 11th century were remarkable for nothing but the number of people embroiled in violence and intrigue in their efforts to gain control of the Punjab and its capital. But then followed the Golden Age of the Ghazni dynasty under the strong and enlightened rule of Ibrahim (c.1059-1099) and his equally effective successor Masud III (1099-1114).

Lahore became principal beneficiary. Ibrahim appointed his grandson, Shirzad, Viceroy of Lahore (1059-1087) and Shirzad made it a leading cultural centre of the Muslim world. The Khangah (scholars' residence), which he founded brought in students and teachers from countries far and near.

Lahore thus rapidly acquired a reputation that ranked after only Baghdad and Ghazni – head of the Empire – among the great Muslim cities. Because of

Above: Faithful shower rupee notes on each other during colourful Thursday evening celebrations at the shrine of Data Ganj Bakhsh, which attracts thousands of worshippers.

Overleaf: On the eve of the Islamic Holy Day, thousands make their devotions at the mosque which marks the shrine of Lahore's mystic Patron Saint, Ali Hajweri – immortalized as Data Ganj Bakhsh. Celebrations are marked by religious music and gifts of food to the poor and needy.

its location in the Muslim vanguard against ever hostile Hindu chiefs, the city was favoured with the rule of the most competent, best educated, accomplished and energetic Governors available. Each vied with his predecessor to bring the city closer to the splendour of the Muslim capital, Ghazni.

Opposite: Traditional buildings in older part of Lahore, where commerce goes on around the clock.

The Viceroy, who maintained an elaborate court, was normally a royal prince of distinction. His officers were Turks, Persians and Afghans of proven loyalty and ability. Intellectuals of the day who wanted to compete with the finest Ghazni "establishment" figures flocked to Lahore as the place in which they could be seen for their own worth and not hidden in the shadow of the acknowledged "great". The poets Masud Razi and his son Abu Farj were among these and Lahore's own Masud bin Sa'ad Salman was counted one of the "top ten" poets in the Persian tongue, the language of culture.

The author of the oldest surviving Persian work on mysticism – Lahore's patron saint, known as Data Ganj Bakhsh – and the scholar-diplomat Imam Hassan al-Sanghani were among the city's numerous prose-writers of renown.

Trade flourished. From Mahmud's time onwards caravans between Lahore and Khurasan had been protected to such effect that a new settlement – possibly today's Lahori Mandi behind the Lahori gate – sprang up. (Local tradition says Malik Ayyaz founded this settlement. The real "Old Lahore" in this tradition, was what's today called Icchra).

In 1099, when Seljuk Turks took Ghazni, Masud III made Lahore his capital.

Though no visible trace remains, many mosques, mausolea, palaces and gardens must have been built in a city of such pre-eminence. A gap in the records leaves it unclear whether Lahore was continuously capital thenceforth, but certainly for Khusrau Shah (1152-1160) it was, and it seems to have retained this eminence to the dynasty's end in 1186.

The last Ghaznivide ruler, Khusrau Malik, (1160-1186) saw Lahore become an even larger city: in 1180 it was so big that 20,000 men, under Shihabuddin Ghuri – better known as Mohamed of Ghor – couldn't take it. Lahore was finally annexed without a drop of blood spilt in battle, after Mohamed captured Malik by a ruse.

Mohamed of Ghor had been sent by his brother, Sultan Ghias-ud-din to annex the provinces which belonged to the now-subverted dynasty of Ghazni. Mohamed's progress was impressive. Rapidly he subdued the whole of the Indus Valley – till he reached Lahore. Twice under Khusrau Malik the capital city successfully defied him, and twice Mohamed was forced to retire.

Mohamed thereupon sent back to Lahore, in triumph and by leisurely marches, Khusrau's son, who had been committed to the court of the Ghor Sultan as a guarantee of Khusrau's good faith. His object now, Mohamed claimed, was to lead his great army against the Seljuk Turks. "He could trust Khusrau."

Overjoyed to learn of his son's safe return Khusrau marched out of Lahore to embrace him; only to discover that the crafty Ghorian general had doubled back by another route and now stood with 20,000 men between him and the city.

Khusrau was compelled to surrender, and Lahore too.

Admiration for the stratagem is tempered by what followed. Allegedly warned by an astrologer, Mohamed murdered Khusrau and all his family, and thus extinguished the Ghaznivide dynasty established by the great Mahmud two centuries before.

Professor Dar feels that contemporary court chroniclers failed to do justice to this period in Lahore's history. Of its buildings little remains: although one shrine – that of Data Ganj Bakhsh "The Saint who dispenses Favours" – has

always been popular with the people of Punjab particularly of Lahore. The original name of this renowned mystic was Ali Mukhdum Hajweri, who in 1039 left his native Ghazni to settle in Lahore. He died in 1072 and was buried close by the mosque he had had built. The tomb, just outside the Bhatti Gate of the old city, attracts hundreds of worshippers every day, especially at sundown on Thursdays, the start of the Muslim holy day. In 1986 a huge new mosque was being built opposite the site.

Three other tombs survive from the same time: that of the Governor Ayyaz – inconspicuous now in the Rang Mahal area of the city, though originally in a garden which surrounded it till the first half of last century; and those of the two Zanjani saints, Shah Hussain and Sayed Yaqub Sadar Diwan. Their tombs too used to be in a garden known as the Zanjani Garden which survived at least until the first half of 17th century.

Two coins are the only other tangible evidence of this period. One, held in the Lahore Museum, was minted in the city of Mahmudpur – believed to have been an early name of Lahore – in the time of Mahmud of Ghazni. His Mint is thought to have stood near the Shalamar Gardens at Mahmud Buti.

Above: Niwin Mosque, one of the city's few pre-Mughal buildings, undergoing restoration work.

Opposite: Modern power lines mar the centuries-old profile of the Bhati Gate, an ancient entrance to the city.

Above: Venerable Punjabi elder.

A second coin, found in Lahore Fort in 1959, was minted in Ghazni in 1025.

The period from Mohamed of Ghor's accession in 1186 to the end of the following century is marked above all by war, intrigue, violence and such rape of Lahore that finally – for 30 years – the former imperial capital was abandoned. It was re-populated, by deliberate policy under Ulugh Khan, in the 1270s.

Not surprisingly praise for heroism in the fight rings constantly through the records of the period, and in the early years Mohamed of Ghor naturally figures prominently.

In conflict with the Hindu Rajputs in the great battle of Narain he attacked from his horse the war elephant of the Rajput General Govind Rai and "with the strength of a lion, in one stroke knocked two of his adversary's teeth down his throat". The Rai, no less resourceful, incapacitated Mohamed by plunging his spear through his arm. "Only through the devotion of a brave young Khiljai warrior, who, clasping his master round the chest, spurred on the horse and bore him from the midst of the fight," was Mohamed's life saved. While he himself was being carried almost insensible the 65 kilometres back to Lahore, many of his lieutenants were scattering, accepting defeat.

Once recovered from his wound Mohamed showed what he thought of that. He ordered them to Ghor and forced them to walk the city wearing the nose-bags of their horses, giving them the "option" of eating the fodder the bags contained or having their shameful heads sabred off.

The records don't say how many stomached their pride.

The Hindu Rajah himself, incidentally, was also accorded praise. "Seven times did this brave representative of the Aryan chivalry carry his arms to the very gates of Lahore." But he was finally defeated and put to death by the Muslim king at Tarain in 1193.

The hill-tribe Ghakkars also constantly over-ran Punjab and even captured Lahore; but they too finally yielded – both to Muslim arms and to the faith of Islam.

Mohamed was cruelly assassinated by a fanatic at Dam Yak near Sohawa in 1206. He had loved Lahore well and spent so much time there it was effectively his winter capital. Now his successor – another former slave – Qutbuddin Aibak had himself crowned in Lahore, and established his throne in the city. He spent most of his too-brief reign resisting the attempts of rivals to grab his throne. He died, much regretted, in 1210 after a fall from his horse while playing Chaugan, a type of polo. He was buried where he fell and died; the event described, somewhat vividly, by the official record: "like a treasure in the bowels of the earth".

A magnificent mausoleum in the middle of a park was erected to his memory, but both mausoleum and park are now lost, though a reconstruction of the monument stands near Anarkali Bazaar.

In 1210, Aram Baksh, Aibak's son, also had himself crowned in Lahore, but a more determined relative, Altutmish, set up a rival throne in Delhi and won the ensuing battle to decide who should prevail. The event marks the end of Lahore's days as imperial capital – apart from a brief period three centuries later – and the beginning of nearly a century of woe for the Queen of cities.

For both the Ghorids and the Mameluks, Slaves, who succeeded them in power, Lahore's importance was almost exclusively strategic – as a buffer against the incessant Mongol invasions. Halfway between Delhi, the seat of the ruler, and Ghazni – the ancient, lost, but emotionally still potent homeland of the dynasty – Lahore was both recruiting-ground and garrison for the famed Turkish mercenaries who, under good leaders, distinguished themselves in keeping the descendants of Genghis Khan's marauders more or less at bay.

It's not clear how well Iltutmish succeeded in protecting Lahore. Some accounts say that in 1221 he diverted the Khan's troops to Sind, and so saved the Punjab; others that Lahore was ravaged at this time. Sadly, there's no doubt about what happened in 1241 in the brief reign of the ineffectual Muizuddin Bahram Shah. The Mongols beseiged Lahore for months, and finally entered the demoralised city unopposed, massacred its inhabitants and left the place desolate. For 30 years hardly anyone inhabited the ruins. Those that did had no more hope of help from Delhi than they had from the Mongols who were now dominant throughout Central Punjab.

Above: Bearded patriarch of ancient Lahore.

In 1266 came relief. Ghiasuddin Balban ascended the Delhi throne and made the restoration of Lahore and all Punjab a priority. He appointed his nephew, Sher Khan, governor: and this man carried the war vigorously to his enemies.

Balban meanwhile repeopled Lahore and its surrounding villages, appointed architects and superintendants to restore the devastated areas, rebuilt the fort, and returned to the province full internal government. He then placed his own son, Prince Mohamed, at the head of the government of Multan and Lahore.

Prince Mohamed appears to have combined both courage and success in battle with a rare appreciation of literature. Poetry was his passion. He would have texts read to him and then listen attentively as learned men discussed the relative merits of the authors.

His greatest delight lay in honouring poets like Amir Khusrow, the poet laureate now regarded as father of Urdu literature. Khusrow was known – presumably for the brilliant plumage of his words – as "the parrot of Hindustan". He was the Prince's constant companion: accompanying him even into battle.

When Samar – "bravest dog of all the dogs of Genghis Khan" – threatened Lahore, Prince Mohamed took to the field, defeated him, and recovered all the territory taken by the invader. After a bloody fight he then expelled a second Mongol force. But then, to the desolation of the whole army, a strong escaping unit of the enemy surprised the Prince "and succeeded in despatching him on the banks of the Ravi". Khusrow was taken prisoner. With difficulty

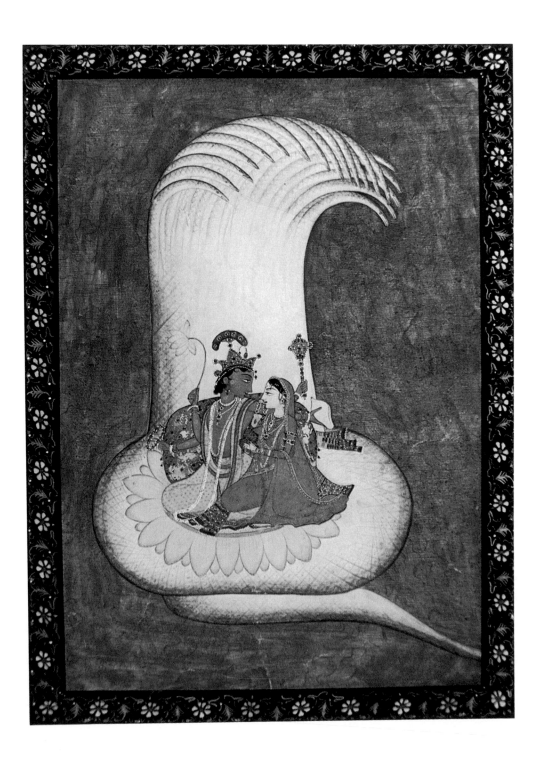

Right: Treasured relic of Lahore Museum's world famous collection of the Kangra paintings depicts a resting Krishna and Radha.

Left: Depiction of Radha and Krishna from the Lahore Museum's collection of Basoli-style art.

his release was negotiated. The elegy he wrote for his patron failed to console Sultan Balban, who – now 80 – "sank under the weight of his grief".

For nearly 250 years Lahore virtually dropped out of historical sight; except for the depressing frequency with which it was attacked, entered, devastated and abandoned.

The Khokhars constantly ravaged the city and Tamurlane alone had the strength to drive them away; only, however, so that he could loot and ravage for himself, undisturbed. His forces settled a suburb of the city – endowing it with the name it still bears: Mughulpura. It was long one of the wealthiest parts of the city, though nothing of its foundations remains.

The Delhi-based rulers – most of them inadequate anyway – treated Lahore through most of this dark period simply as an outpost in their defences against Mongol invasion. The fortress was restored at various times, but the city lacked real security for its inhabitants, who consequently fled the numerous invasions they were powerless to resist.

Lahore's governors did whatever seemed best at the time. Some fled, some parleyed, some betrayed Delhi and abetted the invader, some few resisted: some, at different times, did all.

In 1398 for example Shaikha Khokhar submitted to Tamurlane; only to rebel when he thought himself safe. Tamurlane – "Fire-brand of the Universe" – was not the man to brook that kind of thing. The plunder of the city and the entire

Above: Wheelwright fashions a wagon wheel. Traditional crafts are an enduring feature of Punjabi life.

surrounding country which he ordered as punishment was awesome: from Lahore especially the tally of seized wealth, property and horses seemed endless. "The princes and nobles whom I had sent to Lahore returned from that place bringing with them much wealth and prosperity," Tamurlane noted with evident satisfaction. He was a man who had seen plenty of spoil in his time and was not easily impressed. He certainly didn't want any more for himself. "I divided it among the nobles in attendance at my Court."

The few Lahore Governors who showed character through this period tended to find their way to Delhi, and in Delhi onto the imperial throne. So, in 1321, Ghias-ud-Din Toghlak, son of one of Balban's slaves, having distinguished himself as Viceroy of Lahore under the name Ghazi Khan, founded another dynasty in Delhi which endured most of a century: till 1414.

In that year another Lahore Viceroy, Khizr Khan Syad, took the occasion of the ruler Mahmud Toghlak II's death to march on the capital, evict the newly-installed monarch from the throne and assume the royal diadem himself "in the name of Tamurlane" – a canny piece of psychology in a kingdom restless with ambitious princes. (He also happened to enjoy the advantage of commanding the considerable, and loyal, Punjab army).

But this new Syad dynasty cared nothing for Lahore which again, as ever, was in the vanguard of suffering. In 1421 it was said that no living thing had its abode there 'except the owl of ill-omen'. Syad rule was brief. In 1448 the last of the line, Sultan Ala-ud-din abdicated, calling upon the then Governor of Lahore, Bahlol Lodhi, to come and assume charge of the rapidly shrinking Empire.

It was the end of a period which for Lahore was generally wretched and, during much of which the Khokhars terrorised the region: plundering the cities and villages alike and persecuting their residents. In his efforts to re-populate the city one Emperor was said to have paid people a salary just to live in Lahore!

The Lodhi dynasty which assumed power by invitation in 1448 was weak. Ironically though – and because destiny was to replace them with the massive stability of the great Mughals – they bequeathed to Lahore some of the oldest buildings still standing in the city. The most significant is probably the Niwin Masjid in Dogran Street in the old walled city. From this time, too, date the Madrassah (School) Kala Shah Kaku and the Madrassah Firoz Gilani, and the Khangah (Hospice) of Hazrat Abdul Jalil.

Above: Dervishes whirl through a city market-place.

Opposite top: Long renowned for their hand-knotted carpets, original designs and illustrations, Lahore craftsmen transform silk and wool into masterpieces of the weaver's art.

Above: Woman deftly trims carpet before despatch to buyer.

Left: Hand woven Lahore carpets sell in the United States and Europe for up to $30,000.

The great enduring achievement of these Lodhi, however, was of quite another order. They antagonised one of their Lahore Governors – Dowlat Khan Lodhi – so much that he rebelled and master-minded a conspiracy against them. With other disenchanted Lodhi princes Dowlat Khan asked the ruler of Kabul to invade!

It was a fateful invitation. The ruler at the time was Babur – "The Tiger". And invasion of Hindustan was exactly what he had been contemplating for quite some time.

Opposite bottom: 17th century carpet from the Mughal Shah Jahan's era.

3 Builders of Another Paradise

The great Mughal dynasty – founded by Babur after his successful invasion of the Punjab – delivered Lahore from the ruin and desolation of all the preceding centuries. More, the Mughals set the city on a pedestal so eminent and solid that two subsequent centuries of pillage and destruction could not remove the legacy of architectural and artistic splendour they bequeathed. Under them the Pearl of the Punjab came into her own, became truly a queen among cities and as the greatest of her writer sons, Abu-al-Fazal, claimed with pride: "the grand resort of all nations".

Naturally, the emperors responsible for bringing such distinction to Lahore have been much eulogised. Even today's scholars find them to have been chivalrous, brave, enterprising and imaginative, delightfully humorous, and the most enlightened patrons of literature and fine arts to flourish in the East. Yet, just as powerful as their driving ambition to create, build and sponsor works of enduring strength and surpassing beauty, was their indulgence in savage destruction and at times horrifying cruelty.

This double edge to their personalities is perhaps the most noticeable characteristic shared by Babur and his first five legitimate successors.

Nonetheless, from the renowned cultural centres of Bokhara and Samarkand, scholars, orators and poets flocked to Lahore during their reigns and, encouraged by royal favour, made the city the cultural capital of a mighty empire. Befitting physical improvements followed swiftly: fine gardens were laid out and irrigation introduced on a serious scale; spacious mosques resplendent with mosaic, fresco and stucco work were built; caravanserais, palaces, precious tombs, minarets and imposing park gates erected. Lahore's finest buildings date from this period. Today the city boasts the largest collection of Mughal architecture anywhere: including the very oldest of Mughal relics, the Baradari (Pavilion) built circa 1535 by Kamran, brother to Babur's son and successor, Humayun. Many of the best works of scholarship also date from this period. Culturally Punjab now came to dominate the Empire as Lahore had long dominated the Punjab.

Not only scholars, orators and poets flocked to the brave new Lahore. Kings, princes and courtiers, rich merchants, philosophers and holy men followed suit as the city's wealth, renown and population grew beyond all bounds.

None of this was haphazard. It was conscious Mughal policy. Once again it was the geographical situation of Lahore that pre-determined the role the Mughals entrusted to her.

From the days of Mahmud (998) down to the last of the Lodhis (1526) the Afghan city of Ghazni had dominated the fortunes – and more frequent misfortunes – of Lahore. All the rulers of that time recognised that Delhi was the key to their ambition for wealth and power. Not only were Delhi's riches legendary, but with the mountains behind to north and northeast, and secure lines of communication with Ghazni in the north north-west, from Delhi they

Opposite: Close to the burial place of Emperor Jahangir's favourite antelope, Daulat Khana pavilion dominates Sheikhupura, which was his favourite hunting ground. Known during his day as Jahangirabad, in AD 1607, after the death of Mans Raj, the antelope, Jahangir ordered the building of a tower to mark the burial spot, placed a life-size, red sandstone statue of the animal above the grave and forbade antelope hunting in the area. Excavations in 1959 unearthed the head of the statue.

could concentrate their undivided attention on the control and spread of their rule – towards Bengal in the east and southwards as far as they dared to venture. Lahore, then, lay to the north of the strategic link road between the new – Delhi – and the old – Ghazni – capitals of the Empire. As soon as Delhi was taken the Ghaznivide rulers saw in Lahore generally only a fortress from which to guard the Ghazni-Delhi lifeline further south. Depalpur was on that road and, to the Ghazni dynasties, politically more important for just that reason. Now the arrival in the sub-continent of the warrior Babur shifted the geography of imperial control north. Not only was he of a startling new breed of creative and thinking warrior-lords – to whom the ability to produce was as important as the power and will to destroy – but his base in Kabul swung the axis of approach to Delhi straight through the ancient stronghold, Lahore. This was why Sher Shah Suri wanted Lahore destroyed: because it lay directly on the road an invader from Kabul would follow to reach, and attack, Delhi.

Thus under Babur, in addition to its long-established and pivotal military role, Lahore became politically significant to the Delhi Emperor: for contact with his base, Kabul. The only possible rival on the same road, Peshawar, was too close to Kabul and too far from Delhi. Babur and his successors therefore deliberately dedicated time and resources to making Lahore not just militarily invulnerable but also economically self-supporting and aesthetically worthy of its new dignity. In fact, Lahore became officially the "number two" city in the Empire, with Delhi first as *Darul Khilafat*, Seat of Power, Lahore *Darul Sultanat*, Seat of Empire, and Agra, nearer Delhi, *Darul Adl*, Seat of Judgement.

It's not surprising that, besides the resident royalty, the wealthy merchants and the admired intelligentsia, many a newcomer to Hindustan and retiring civil servant chose Lahore as the city to live in – especially as people from the west all found Lahore much more congenial to their taste than the hotter, drier, less hospitable Delhi. Babur had some quite caustic comment on just this.

Of the great Mughals' love for Lahore there can be no doubt. The three greatest – Akbar the Great, Jahangir and Shah Jahan – favoured it especially. Jahangir, in accord with his last will, is buried in Lahore; his son Shah Jahan was born there; Jahangir's remarkable wife, Nur Jahan, famous for beauty, culture and the strength of her passionate will, chose to live her last widowed 18 years in the city. She too is buried there, near her husband; as is her brother – Shah Jahan's Prime Minister and father of the noble lady Mumtaz Mahal (for whom Shah Jahan built the matchless Taj Mahal in Agra), and the Empire's greatest engineer Ali Mardan Khan, builder of the Royal Canal, central feature of the city's incomparable Shalamar Gardens. Each of these was honoured with a magnificent tomb in the city.

The buildings they commanded for the city illustrate its importance to them. Architecturally, today's Lahore virtually starts with them. Only a

Opposite: The grand entrance to Badshahi Mosque faces the monumental Alamgiri gate across an ancient garden court. The tablet over the porchway in Naskh characters records that it was built in AD 1674 by Fidai Khan, Aurangzeb's foster-brother and 'Master of Engineers'. The gate was subsequently moved to bring it into line with the entrance to the mosque.

Opposite: Tomb of Sharfun Nisa Begum, sister of an 18th century Lahore Governor. Because of its decoration it's known as the Sarvwala Maqbara, or Cypress

Mausoleum. The burial chamber inside the tower where, every day during her lifetime the Begum spent an hour reading the Qu'ran, is about five metres above the

ground. Her copy of the Holy Book and a sword set with precious stones were buried with her, but the tomb was robbed during the Sikh period.

Above: One hundred and fifty fountains surround a platform in the Shalamar Gardens, where musicians and dancers entertained the Emperor Shah Jahan after he built the gardens in AD 1642. Laid out on three ascending terraces, the gardens are unified by hundreds of fountains and water channels.

handful of earlier structures survive. Following the earliest remaining Mughal building – Kamran's Baradari, already noted – came the crucial undertaking by Akbar to rebuild and enlarge the city's ancient mudbrick citadel into the awesome brick and stone fortress that stands today. The Akbari Gate and large sections of wall are exactly as he built them.

Jahangir and Shah Jahan lavishly adorned the interior with mosques, gardens, palaces, audience halls, and courtyards with fountains and flower gardens. They also added to the fort what must have been a unique and magnificent *tour de force* – the 745 square metres of picture wall west and north of the Shah Burj. The superb effect these faience mosaics must have conveyed originally – especially as reflected in the waters of the river Ravi which, in early Mughal days, flowed immediately under the castle walls like a moat – is easy to imagine.

Akbar's wife, Maryam Zamani, the mother of Jahangir, ordered the building of the mosque which bears her name and stands close by – the oldest surviving Mughal mosque of known date.

The last of the great Mughals, Aurangzeb, gave Lahore the world's largest mosque, the Badshahi, opposite the stupendous Alamgiri Gate which he

40

Opposite: The tomb which legend says is that of the young girl Anarkali, whom Emperor Akbar saw favour his son, Prince Salim, with a smile and thus had her immured alive. Scholars now say Anarkarli –

Pomegranite Bud – never existed and that Jehangir built this handsome monument for a favourite daughter.

added to the Fortress at the same time.

The old city's walls were Mughal.

Princes and Princesses followed the example of Emperors and their wives, adding *mohallas*, localities, of their own to the city, each adorned with its own *haveli*, elaborate house – unfortunately, in their case, too elaborate to survive. None can now be traced.

From this period also probably date the rich suburbs founded by the wealthy: Icchra, Begumpura, Shahdara and Baghbanpura.

Mughal mosques are generally larger and more elaborate than others, as well as being decorated to a degree that's actually alien to classical mosque design. Without exception all were embellished with graceful arches and minarets and splendid domes. As with the mausolea, park gates and palaces, their decoration was both elaborate and varied: with stone-carving, stone-inlay, pietra-dura, fresco-painting, stucco tracery, mosaic tiles, carved and imitation bricks, carved and painted wooden doors, glass-work, and – specific to Lahore – the glazing of silica-and-lime-based tiles.

One of Lahore's most appealing titles is "city of gardens". The visitor is quickly delighted to find this is no cliche. Gardens mattered to the Mughals –

Above: Fact or fiction, the tragic Anarkali love story has been told in art, verse, drama and dancing. Theatregoers at Lahore's modern Al-Hamra Arts Centre are enthralled by a new play based on the legend.

whether for recreation, ornament, the cultivation of fruit and flowers, or for sheer pleasure. The reason is easy to find in Babur's writings:

"The country has few pleasures to recommend it. The people are not handsome...They have no good horses, no good fish, no grapes or musk-melons, no good fruits, no ice or cold water, no good food and bread in their bazaars, no baths or colleges... In their buildings they study neither elegance nor climate nor appearance nor regularity."

Babur was one of the most refined men of his time; which means he had had the benefit of Persian influence on his upbringing and education. Among many things he did not like about Hindustan was that it was horribly hot and dry. Constantly sounding through his record is how much he misses the cool air and fresh clean water of his native land, together with the order and the repose that come with them.

The Mughal gardens were the Mughal answer to these shortcomings.

They were carefully planned with the twin objectives of protecting their occupants from the intolerable heat and dust, and providing them with facilities for refined and profitable relaxation. Central to this achievement was the provision of efficient and decorative canals – to irrigate the land for trees, fruit and flowers to grow – and an abundance of fountains to cool and refresh the sun-filled air. To be effective, irrigation had to be regular and in straight lines: and this suited the formal geometric designs typical of Islamic architecture. Walls – ensuring privacy and safety – completed these rectangular oases of cool relaxation.

Only on a hot, dry day can the visitor really appreciate the compliment to Lahore represented by the title "City of Gardens". Numerous and beautiful, they are among the city's finest delights.

In Lahore, as elsewhere in the Empire, the Mughals patronized arts and crafts. Akbar the Great (1556-1605) established ateliers for painting, calligraphy, book-binding and heraldry. Once again whatever the Mughals achieved in art and literature – and it was much – may safely be credited to the Punjab in general and to Lahore especially.

The Emperors fostered growth of the textile industry by setting up imperial carpet factories. From a synthesis of Persian, Central Asian, Chinese and Indian they elaborated the unique Mughal style. Three of these imperial workshops were outstanding: those in Agra and Mirzapur and the one in Lahore, where the industry reached its high-point of quality under Shah Jahan. Lahore's factory was also renowned for its luxury tailoring, above all for its expertise in gold and silver thread work, brocades and velvets.

Significantly, the last battles to save the Empire from Afghan subversion, the Maratha rising and Sikh militarism were all fought by forces from Lahore. When, in the late 18th century, Lahore fell to Sikh rule the last hope of saving the Mughal power itself was lost.

Before that sad outcome however the citizens of Lahore enjoyed an

Opposite: Four-towered entrance to the gardens laid out in AD 1646, possibly by Shah Jahan as a gift for a daughter. Though the gardens no longer exist, and Chamburji gate is much defaced, enough remains to demonstrate its original magnificence.

unprecedented span of 181 years of peace and prosperity during which their rulers established an empire recognised as one of the greatest that ever presided over the destiny of an Asiatic country.

Lahore today – poorer than it should be in the range of its mosques, palaces and gardens, and sadly deprived, in many of those that stand, of the incomparable wealth of artistic embellishment in which they once gloried – presents to the visitor nonetheless an ancient city centre unique in southern Asia. It's the most powerful evidence of the favour shown to Lahore during those first two fabulous centuries of Mughal rule.

Ironically the man who founded this rightly renowned dynasty – the Turkish-speaking Tiger, or Babur – himself directly contributed nothing but anguish to the city that was to become the favourite resort of so many of his descendants. His first four day visit there was dedicated to punitive burning, looting and destruction on a scale that compared with that perpetrated by his ancestor Tamurlane, laconically said to have "laid waste Lahore" on his way to conquering Delhi.

Unlike that 1398 visitation, however, Babur's presaged an investment in the future – the start of a totally new chapter in the city's history.

With amazing swiftness the fires which Babur set were to forge Lahore's incomparable Golden Age – which even in the final decades of the 20th century, and despite many ravages, gleams still.

BABUR THE TIGER

Left: Portrait of the Mughal Emperor Babur in the Faqir Khana Family Museum.

ODD MAN OUT

For many people Babur's son Humayun (1508-1556) hardly belongs among the first six Mughals. They list him only for reasons of chronology.

Humayun inherited all his father's sensitivity, his weakness for opium – his death occurred in 1556 when, after an overdose, he fell down the steep steps of his Delhi observatory and split his skull – and none of his decisiveness. Alone among the early Mughals, Humayun was no man of action.

As soon as he knew of Babur's death the younger son, Mirza Kamran, governor of Kabul and Kandahar, moved to Lahore to make his own bid for power. But the man Babur appointed to rule Lahore – Mir Yunis Ali – remained loyal to Humayun; so Mirza Kamran withdrew, and resorted to the kind of ruse typical of the period. "Denouncing" one of his nobles he expelled him from his camp. The nobleman and his company betook themselves to Lahore city, where poor Mir Yunis Ali was quite taken in. Within days the guests he had welcomed had locked him up and taken control. In Agra, Humayun bowed to the *fait accompli* and made his younger brother ruler of the Punjab as well as of Kabul and Kandahar.

Through the years Humayun was rewarded by Kamran with frequent acts of treachery, but citing his father's admonition he always forgave – allowing Kamran to live to betray another day. Finally however even Humayun had enough. He put out his brother's eyes and sent him to live the rest of his days in Makha.

This Kamran seems to have resembled Babur more than Humayun did. Unlike his older brother he never hesitated about making a decision – though since he never allowed considerations of loyalty to Humayun to get in the way it was doubtless easier for him. He displayed, too, typical Mughal creativity. His rule in Lahore was marked by construction of beautiful gardens and palaces. One extended from the Naulakha, near today's Railway Station, to the river Ravi: then flowing nearby. The ruins of another can still be visited.

Thanks to a 16th century change in the course of the river Ravi these remains are now marooned on an island and – for the privilege of walking where Humayun entertained his guests in a *baradari*, pavilion, set in the middle of a garden pool and seeing, in fact, the foundations of the architectural greatness to come – it's well worth making the short journey out of Lahore to the new Ravi bridge and for a few rupees hiring the services of a boatman to take you there. The river looks deceptively idle here; it's actually dangerous with currents and reeds that take a yearly toll of those who try to swim it. In flood it has changed course several times through the years, imperilling the city in the 17th century, and now – it is said – threatening to undermine the oldest of all Mughal remains.

A more substantial opponent to Humayun was Sher Shah Suri: he who at death's door lamented not having destroyed Lahore. He defeated Humayun in battle in 1540, founded the famous strategic fortress of Rohtas to defend Lahore's northern approaches, and from his capital, Agra, encouraged trade links between Punjab via Peshawar with central Asia, and Punjab via Lahore with China. He linked Lahore and Multan with a road – and for the benefit of travellers had fruit trees planted at regular intervals along the 2,500 kilometre road between the river Nilab and Bengal. His death in 1545 is lamented by historians who declare him one of the region's greatest rulers.

Not surprisingly, in view of his ambivalent attitude to the city, Lahore bears no architectural testimony to his five year reign.

His son Islam Shah Suri is credited by some with the building of a small three-domed mosque which can be found in the western wall of the so-called Akbari Serai near the mausoleum of Jahangir at Shahdara, across the river, not far from Kamran's island *Baradari*.

Humayun himself, evicted from his empire by Sher Shah Suri in 1540, spent 14 years on the run. He managed to retain the loyalty of a small band of followers, including two other brothers, and married the 14-year-old daughter of one of their spiritual advisers. She bore him Akbar the Great.

Humayun finally returned to power in Delhi with a powerful army provided by the rulers of Persia – who apparently saw his re-instatement as a way of extending their sphere of influence.

Some writers say his tomb in Delhi, beautiful and imposing, is quite out of proportion to his significance. Humayun nonetheless holds two high titles to recognition. First, however ingloriously he achieved it, he handed on to his son most of the empire he had inherited, lost for 14 years, and regained the year before his death; second, the son to whom he delivered that empire, by his child wife, Hamida Begum, was Akbar – almost universally regarded as the greatest of all Mughal emperors.

AKBAR THE GREAT

The 13-year-old boy who inherited the elements of Empire from his ill-fated father, Humayun, was destined to acquire spectacular ascendancy not only over the whole of south Asia – from Persia, Afghanistan and modern Pakistan in the west, through Kashmir in the north to the Bay of Bengal in the east, and thence down through much of south India – but over the Mughal dynasty itself.

Humayun had appointed him Governor of the Punjab only a few months before the fatal observatory fall, and the heir to the throne was *en route* with his mentor – a general of renown, Bairam Khan – when news of Humayun's death reached them at Kalanaur. Akbar (1542-1605) was crowned forthwith, and the Khan, in accordance with Humayun's will, became Regent.

In the years leading up to his own assumption of full personal control of the Mughal Empire at the age of 18 Akbar learned much, both about dealing with rebellion – especially in the Punjab – and about the handling of men to secure maximum control.

He had formidable natural talents for the task. Despite his short build he was physically powerful, even more than the legendary Babur. He was ruthless. Enraged by the intrigues of a foster-brother he struck him down with his fist and ordered him literally thrown from the city walls – twice, because the first time didn't kill.

According to legend, when Akbar saw his son, Prince Salim – the future Jahangir – smiling at one of the beautiful dancers in his harem he suspected them of having a secret affair and had the girl built into the city wall alive.

This was the famous Anarkali – Pomegranate Bud – and the story ends, to the satisfaction of romantics, if not of historians, with her presumed lover, Jahangir, subsequently building the imposing monument which still bears her name, at the site of her execution.

Inscriptions inside the tomb are now said to indicate that the tomb was actually the burial-place of Jahangir's wife Sahib-i-Jamal, who died in 1599. Historians in fact now say there never existed a lady of Anarkali's name or character.

Above: Stylized animal figure on a corbel overlooking Jahangir's quadrangle. Animal representations emphasize the charming simplicity of the ruler's red sandstone courtyard, but suggest he was influenced by non-Muslim art forms.

This dignified yet relaxed-looking balcony in white marble projected from the southern side of the building, supported on brackets of red sandstone. The modern visitor cannot help reflecting that the great Mughals must have felt very secure to step out onto it to present themselves so publicly. No modern Head of State could – unless effectively screened from view by masses of milling security officials. Yet there enthroned, the Mughal Emperors daily received eminent visitors and guests, or watched as their superbly groomed horses and caparisoned elephants paraded past. Europeans who witnessed the ceremonial were astonished at its grandeur and magnificence.

The flat roof above the Daulat Khan-i-Khas-o-Aam, with its Mughal watch-tower, gives a superb view of Jehangir's quadrangle below. Although it bears the name of his son, this lovely area too was in fact begun by Akbar.

A curious water-tank was built in the Fort at this time; apparently such that its floor gave entry to a perfectly dry and beautifully furnished and equipped dining room: another example of the fascination novelties held for the tirelessly energetic mind of this ruler.

A Persian inscription over the north and east doors of a beautiful little mosque opposite Akbar's gate to the Fort records that this building, the oldest surviving dated mosque in Lahore, was constructed on the orders of Akbar's queen, Jahangir's mother, Maryam Zamani. It is now named after her.

In the 19th century, under Sikh rule, it was used as a powder magazine, but it was restored to the Muslims in 1850. It remains remarkable for its dome and its frescos which elaborately interlace floral and geometric designs with Qu'ranic inscriptions in Naskh characters. Today they are considered the finest Mughal frescos anywhere.

During this time Lahore was home to generals, wealthy leaders of commerce, saints, philosophers, poets and musicians. "It is a very populous city," commented Abu-al-Fazal in 1557, "the resort of people of all nations and a centre of extensive commerce. In the shortest time great armies can be collected there and ammunitions of war in any quantity can be procured for the use of troops." Abu-al-Fazal was Akbar the Great's Prime Minister, and a scholar whose stylish writings won universal admiration as "model and despair of the Age". A royal Mint, a carpet factory and many other institutions were founded.

For his Lahore gardens the Emperor sent to Persia for experts to cultivate the grape and melon in the city. The city itself was run by 12 of the ablest people in Akbar's court, Punjab was counted the most important province in the Empire, and from now on, even when Lahore was not itself imperial capital, the governor of Punjab ranked higher than the Prime Minister of the Empire.

Culturally the city rose to new and splendid heights. Akbar brought to

Lahore the most distinguished scholars, writers, poets, musicians and thinkers of the day, ordered histories to be written, epics translated and illustrations made. He encouraged research.

His curiosity was endless – leading on at least one occasion to the discomfiture of a charlatan who made money by tricking people into believing he could cross the river Ravi unseen and instantaneously. All he did was to have his son – whose voice was indistinguishable from his own – call out from the far side the moment he had hidden himself on the near. Akbar ordered a private demonstration of the "miracle", and when the man fell silent, threatened he'd throw him into the river from the top of the castle with hands and feet bound to see what sort of miracle could save him. The threat produced a full confession and – although the sequel is not told – presumably the end of an apparently lucrative little fraud.

Above: Glittering pietra dura inlay of semi-precious stones –lapis-lazuli, onyx, cornelian, jaspar and topaz – studs the floor of the sculpted fountain pool in the Diwan-i-Khas pavilion of Shah Jahan's courtyard. Though the first use of this inlay is attributed to Jahangir, few examples rival this work for sheer refinement.

Right: Mughal miniature depicting the Emperor Jahangir giving audience, one of the Lahore Museum collection.

Maulana Mohamed Amin of Lahore in terms hardly to be expected from a previously notorious rake:

"Notwithstanding his wordly connections, he is distinguished by independence of character and contentment, and has command over his spirit. I was much pleased with his society."

In Agra, too busy with affairs to leave the city but anxious to consult Mian Mir – known as the Saint of Lahore – he invited the holy man to visit him in the capital. "Truly he is the beloved of God," Jahangir wrote after the meeting. "In sanctity and purity of soul he has no equal in this age. This humble servant (Jahangir's description of himself) used to go to the saint, who explained to him many minute points of theology. It was my desire to make him an offer of money; but as he was above worldly things I dared not make the offer, and contented myself with the presentation of the skin of an antelope, to serve as a mat for offering prayers."

A royal antelope features in of one of the best-known stories about Jahangir. His passion for hunting dated from childhood. As a young man he spent so much time at the chase outside Lahore that his favoured hunting-ground there came to be called Jahangirabad (the modern Sheikhupura). In the second year of his reign a royal antelope which had taken his fancy, and which he called "Mans Raj", died.

The Emperor had a handsome monument raised over its remains, on which a life-size stone statue of the animal was placed. A stone slab attached to the monument bore a Persian inscription engraved in the handwriting of Mulla Mohamed Hussain Kashmiri, famous for his calligraphy, and Jahangir ordered that no Hindu or Muslim should thenceforth hunt deer within the limits of the place.

Subsequently he ordered a palace to be built in Jahangirabad, with a tank and tower. They stand there still – though considerably modified by the Emperor's son, Shah Jahan.

Jahangir's record of a visit there is interesting: "The tank laid out is large and delightful. In the midst of it is an edifice highly pleasing and attractive...The hunting ground is truly worthy of kings. We stayed here on Friday and Saturday and amused ourselves with hunting of different kinds...One stage away is the garden of Momin, the Ishqbaz, on the banks of the Lahore river. The royal camp was pitched at this spot. There are in this garden fine plants and tall and graceful cypress trees with a beautiful mango plantation. On the 5th of Moharram, having taken our royal seat on the elephant called Indar, we left the garden of Momin and, scattering money by way of Nisar (sacrifice) we marched to the city." A remarkable personality, who could write like this – and impale 700 fellow-men alive!

Like his father Jahangir had a special liking for Lahore and the surrounding region, and while he reigned – apart from the brief period of Khusrow's rebellion – the Punjab enjoyed an extended period of peace and prosperity. He built several palaces and administrative blocks in the Fort for himself – of which the so-called Jahangir's quadrangle survives.

Jahangir's quadrangle – begun in fact by his father – is an enchanting section of the Fort interior. Most of the area is occupied by a large garden, laid out in geometric beds about a central tank containing more than 30 fountains. On the east and west a series of porticoed lodges in red sandstone, with richly carved columns and elaborate brackets sculpted to the forms of elephants, lions and other animals, reveals the influence which Hindu art had upon Jahangir and Akbar. On the north side, overlooking the northern wall of the city below, is Jahangir's own sleeping chamber, known now as Bari Khawabgah. The frontage is a modern reconstruction but the

Overleaf: Jahangir's red sandstone tomb inlaid with white marble, set in an immense garden that was once the property of the Emperor's formidable Queen, Nur Jahan. Historians disagree as to whether she, or Jahangir's son and successor Shah Jahan, had the mausoleum built. During the Sikh period the structure suffered considerably. The British undertook its restoration in 1889.

Shah Jahan's court is smaller and conveys a totally different effect from the larger, adjacent, Jahangir quadrangle. Above all there is something friendly about the porticoes which face out onto Jahangir's fountains, and the red sandstone animals carrying the cross beams of the buildings speak inevitably to the child in everyone. By contrast Shah Jahan's court, in purest marble, is all grace.

The superb *Diwan-i-Khas*, Hall of Private Audience, on the north is an arched pavilion, all white but for the *pietra dura* embellishment of the parapet, and the floor: of multi-coloured marble arranged in geometric patterns. A delightful marble fountain plays in its centre, inlaid with *pietra dura*. The ceiling too is of marble, while latticed marble screens of magnificent craftsmanship adorn the north side.

Opposite, on the south side of the court, lie Shah Jahan's sleeping chambers, *Khawabgah*. Originally porticoed, this five-room building retains the white marble door frames, the dado of the three main rooms and beautiful latticed screens, again in white marble, on the southern wall. Sikh frescos and tracery here conceal Shah Jahan's original decoration.

West of the Khawabgah lie the ruins of Shah Jahan's *Hamman*, Royal Bath. It copied Turkish style – with hot bath, cold bath and dressing room. Most of the chequered marble flooring has gone, but evidence of the complex heating system remains. The Hamman was also used as a Council Chamber, to which only high-ranking nobles were admitted.

On the northwest corner a summer pavilion – the Lal Burj – is two-thirds Shah Jahan; the top storey is Sikh. To judge by the gilded and painted

Their six metre breadth and 65-metre extent were specifically designed to accommodate elephants, carrying members of the royal family and ladies of the Harem. The steps are of brick and the high walls either side are painted to look brick-like. Arrivals and departures were proclaimed by heralds stationed in the west wall galleries.

The Shah Burj itself – originally one, but divided with a wall by the Sikhs – is entered via a marble door decorated with frescoed flower paintings. The first building seen is the Sikh *Athdara* – or Edifice of Eight Doorways – used by Ranjit Singh as a *Kachehri*, Court of Justice. It is decorated with frescos of Krishna celebrating the Spring Festival.

The second court is entirely of marble. To the north is the half-octagon Burj itself, one of the most profusely decorated monuments of the whole Mughal period, and used as his residence by the Emperor when he stayed in Lahore. It was here that the Treaty of Lahore which put an end to Sikh rule in the Punjab and made the territory over to the British was signed on 26 December, 1845.

In this room too, according to the Pakistan Tourism Development Corporation's official guide book, the Koh-i-Noor diamond – now resplendent among the British crown jewels – was handed over to the British. It had belonged to the Mughal Emperors and was estimated to weigh more than 229 carats.

Dr. Dar – quoting S.M. Latif – notes that the Sikh ruler Ranjit Singh forced Shah Shuja-ul-Mulk of Kabul to surrender the huge stone in the Mubarak Haveli in the walled city. The diamond in fact changed hands many times before the British acquired it, so perhaps both accounts are true.

The large central room, richly studded with round and convex mirrors – and

Above: Classic example of pietra-dura inlay in Lahore Fort's Naulakha Pavilion.

Opposite: Shish Mahal or Palace of Mirrors, the large central room of Shah Jahan's Lahore residence in the Fort. The ceiling is Mughal: the walls Sikh. In this hall, on 26 December 1845, the Treaty of Lahore was ratified, ending Sikh rule in the Punjab. Some say it was here, too, that the world's largest known diamond – the Koh-i-Nur, or Mountain of Light, weighing over 229 carats – was handed over to British authorities.

hence called the *Shish Mahal*, Palace of Mirrors, is decorated with *pietra dura* inlay and Sikh frescos. It is carried, on superbly worked double columns, across five handsomely scalloped arches. The ceiling is Mughal, the walls – with their minute pieces of blue and white porcelain – Sikh. Nine smaller rooms adjoin the central hall, all of them decorated with marquetry ceilings. The back wall – like those of the main buildings in Shah Jahan's court – is embellished with marble screening of extraordinary beauty, carved with geometrical and floral designs.

The Burj courtyard is floored with a variety of marbles and the central pool designed to give an impression of waves. The Burj itself is completed by a Belvedere overlooking the city and clearly visible from outside the fort. Unfortunately its condition is bad.

One final structure has to be mentioned before we leave this section of Shah Jahan's creations inside the fort: the Bungla or Naulakha. To some it's the most charming edifice in the fort: a marble pavilion remarkable for the purity of its stone, the intricacy of its decoration – in a single small flower there are over a hundred pieces of tiny, semi-precious stones – and most obviously for its "Bengali-style", downward curving roof. Yet another marvellous marble screen forms the rear wall of this Bungla, which the ladies of the Harem are said to have favoured for the view it gave them of the outside world while they themselves remained hidden.

South of Jahangir's Quadrangle the *Diwan-i-Aam*, Hall of Public Audiences, was commissioned by Shah Jahan to replace the awnings previously used to shelter dignitaries attending the Emperor's daily appearances in the Jharoka. It took three years to build. The large open hall – 56 metres long, 18 broad, and 11 high – stands on a larger rectangular platform: itself edged by a decorative railing in red sandstone like the 40 lofty pillars which support the arches that carry the roof. Traces of another railing, in white marble, can also be seen between the pillars at the hall's outer limits. According to travellers these balustrades separated the various ranks of dignitaries attending the audiences. The huge platform is surrounded by the yet bigger Diwan-i-Aam quadrangle, now dedicated entirely to open gardens, but once surrounded by vaulted apartments, with gateways in the middle of the east, west and south sides.

When Sikh Maharajah Ranjit Singh died his body lay in state in this hall. In the civil war which followed the fort was bombarded by cannon balls fired from minarets of the Badshahi Mosque. The Diwan-i-Aam roof was shattered and the hall collapsed. The building seen today is a British restoration which was used by them as a hospital.

Although considerably diminished from its former glory the Diwan-i-Aam is nonetheless one of the most evocative areas of the Fort. In this airy arcade it's not too difficult to see and hear still the multi-coloured ranks of nobility, ambassadors and state envoys assembled here – to each his proper place designated by smoothly efficient, sometimes officious, ministers of protocol – in excited, maybe fearful anticipation of the grand entry of the Emperor of Hindustan, descendant of Babur, Tamurlane and Genghis, the great and terrible Mughal: Shah-in-Shah, the King of Kings.

It was in this Diwan-i-Aam quadrangle in May 1959 that excavations were carried out. After digging through 20 stratified layers the workmen reached virgin soil some 15 metres down. The upper layers, British and Sikh, contained re-used fired bricks, and showed structures with wide foundations. Then came evidence of Mughal building: a period of intense construction "of solid and massive kind". Next a two-metre thick layer of debris was mixed with fallen mud-bricks, pottery and oil lamps. It showed heavy disturbance, and it was here that the Sultan Mahmud coin already mentioned was found. A three-and-a-half metre high mud-brick wall at this level may have been part of an earlier, pre-Muslim fort's defences. Debris associated with it suggests long and continued occupation.

Lahore's Fort at that time was of crucial importance to the various contenders for power – Muslim versus Hindu, Ghaznivid ruler against local rivals. Already, therefore, the 1959 excavations made contact with the days of the great Sultan Mahmud and the city's patron saint Data Ganj Bakhsh, of the early poets of the city and their patrons, of the period when Lahore was capital of the later Ghaznavid rulers, and with the Fort used for the coronations of their immediate successors.

It's an intriguing thought as one wanders by this ancient site that a dozen or so metres beneath one's feet may lie fascinating new evidence of these watershed centuries in the sub-continent's history.

In 1639 Ali Mardan Khan – a Persian nobleman and Governor of Lahore – proposed to the Emperor that he should call upon the services of expert canal engineers to bring the waters of the river Ravi from Rajpur to Lahore. Shah Jahan approved, and within two years the 160 kilometres long Royal Canal – Shah Nahar – was completed. The Emperor then launched one of his most popular undertakings – the design and construction of the Shalamar Gardens. He ordered another nobleman, Khalilullah Khan, to select the site. The foundations were laid on 12 July that year and less than 18 months later, on 31 October 1642, the Emperor paid his first state visit to the newly completed grounds.

The Shalamar Gardens – six kilometres northeast of the city on the Grand Trunk Road – embody the perfection of landscape architecture demanded by the Mughals. "A garden," Babur wrote, "is the purest of human pleasures." A single visit to Shalamar shows just what he meant.

Lavishly spread over three descending terraces the gardens are unified by water which runs down the six metre wide central canals and their various offshoots and reservoirs, and through the countless fountains.

The highest and lowest of the three terraces are 265 metre squares. Each is divided into quarters by water channels which – decorated with fountains in red sandstone and marble – run north-south and east-west.

In the centre of these terraces – where the channels intersect – larger pools with more fountains accentuate the cool freshness of the air.

The original name for the top terrace, *Farah Bakhsh*, Bestower of Pleasure, suggests that its gardens were planted with flowers and sweet-scented shrubs; *Faiz Bakhsh*, Bestower of Plenty, name for the lower level, suggests this was planted with fruit-bearing trees and plants.

The higher terrace was reserved exclusively for the Harem and ladies of the Imperial Court. A marble screen, where the red sandstone balustrade now runs, secured their privacy.

The central terrace – an oblong 265 metres wide but only 78 long – is especially elaborate. It is divided lengthwise into three: the middle section raised and containing the great tank, over 60 metres across, with more than a hundred fountains, four pavilions, and – one of the Gardens' most splendid features – the great cascade. This large, white marble wedge carries the water down from the top terrace level to the central tank over a sculpted surface which artfully gives the impression of brilliantly cascading diamonds.

By this cascade the poetess Princess Zebun-Nisa – daughter of the last of the great Mughals, Aurangzeb – wrote her Persian poems. One of special beauty suggests the impression made by the cascade on a broken heart:

"O waterfall! for whose sake art thou weeping?
In whose sorrowful recollection hast thou wrinkled thy brows?
What pain was it that impelled thee, like myself, the whole
night
To strike thy head against stone and to shed tears?"

At the foot of the cascade is the Emperor's marble throne. Either side of the central pool are pavilions, originally of red sandstone, from which one can walk a causeway to the platform in the middle of the great tank. This was specifically designed for evening relaxation, and it's easy to imagine the delight of sitting out here with friends at the end of day under a clear moonlit sky, in quiet conversation among the playing fountains.

The side sections of the central terrace are dedicated to roses.

Nowadays – the opposite of the original concept – you enter the Gardens at the level of the highest terrace. Two great portals in the corners of the wall at the bottom end of the Gardens used to be the access points; and progress was upwards, so that each level was revealed – a delightful surprise – as it was reached.

Numerous other features – pavilions, sleeping quarters, private and public audience halls, a bath house, gateways and towers – adorn these wonderful Gardens. They are also surrounded by high walls with serrated battlements, though these could not save the Gardens from serious vandalism once the power and authority of the Emperors declined after Aurangzeb's death. Much marble was looted for buildings in Amritsar and elsewhere. The canals and tanks were filled in and the entire garden put under the plough. Ranjit Singh was both the worst offender, and – once securely in power – their preserver. He ordered massive restoration work, re-dug the canals and tanks and plastered over the buildings from which marble had been removed.

Today, if not in their full glory, the Gardens are nonetheless an unfailing joy which possibly more than anywhere else in Lahore give an idea of the stature and refinement of the Mughals' remarkably creative minds. At the same time, for knowing so well how to create this "purest of human pleasures", they seem more human and agreeable than their other, grosser acts at times make them appear.

Shah Jahan is also credited by some with completing the mausoleum of his father. He certainly ordered one fitting the dignity of his father-in-law and Prime Minister, Yaminud Daula Asaf Khan. In the nearby Hiran Minar he ordered construction of new buildings, "to be achieved within twelve months".

As always the royal building example was followed closely by leading ministers and top soldiers. Governor Wazir Khan built what's now considered the most magnificent mosque of any period in South Asia. The exterior of this fine building is splendidly colourful with mosaics on the face and frescos on the entrance interiors. The powerful Persian influence upon the Mughals – clearly visible here – is ascribed to the impact of Humayun's wanderings upon him. Shah Jahan actually sent for leading Persian artists who supervised the work of local craftsmen. This is evident at the Wazir Khan Mosque – in the

Opposite: Dai Anga Mosque, built by Shah Jahan's wet-nurse and named after her, stands near the main railway station and is remarkable for its small, enamelled faience tiles. The Sikhs used it as a powder magazine: the British as a residence. It was returned to Muslims in 1903.

geometric forms, the formality of the floral design and the calligraphy. The rigidity of mind which sometimes went with this approach is also evident: the texts quoted on each side of the mosque are identical.

The same Wazir commissioned work on a unique Date Grove, *Nakhla Wazir Khan*. Its magnificent central pavilion suffered from neglect but is now being restored. He also erected smaller mosques, bazaars and palaces. Two of them survive in the walled city: one inside Tibbi Bazaar, another inside Taxali Gate.

Associated with the designing and building going on all over the city were practitioners of many arts and crafts: painting, stone-carving and inlay, mosaics, and glasswork. The Emperor's Carpet Factory in Lahore won such renown that compared with its products those of the King of Persia were said to resemble coarse canvas! All the rooms of the Royal Fort were furnished with carpets from this super-factory. (Lahore Museum shows an example of its work).

Although his outstanding strength lay in building, Shah Jahan loved books and learning too, and Lahore in his time was noted especially for the number of its saints and mystics – men like Mian Mir, Shah Bilawal Qadri and others.

The fifth Mughal was stricter in religious matters than his predecessors. He took back from the Christian missionaries the permission his father had given to practise openly. When in Lahore he would always visit the holy men of the city. Nonetheless he was wise and enlightened in his approach to religion. He would surely never have committed the grievous tactical error his son Aurangzeb made in enforcing the letter of the law of Sharia, in the way he did – which led to the final alienation of the Empire's majority Hindu population.

Shah Jahan's was a truly magnificent reign. Never was the Mughal Empire so prosperous or secure. An early account of a visit to Lahore gives a vivid impression:

"On the 9th, Wazir Khan presented his Majesty with jewels, gold and silver utensils, rich stuffs, carpets, horses and camels, valued at four lakhs of rupees, which he had collected during the period of his vice-royalty in the Punjab. The same day, Said Khan, Subedar of Kabul, having had the honour of an audience, presented his majesty with one thousand Ashrafis, one hundred horses and one hundred camels. Kalich Khan, governor of Multan, made a present of 18 horses of Irak, together with curiosities of Persia. Mahabat Khan, Faujdur of Kangra, was promoted, and other Subedars similarly honoured. The whole of the presents amounted to ten lakhs of rupees. On the 15th his Majesty visited the mausoleum of Jahangir and distributed rupees ten thousand to the poor, while rupees five thousand were distributed to the princes who accompanied him. His Majesty, who entertained much respect for the fakirs, paid a visit to the saint, Mian Mir. His Majesty, knowing that he cared not for worldly wealth, presented him with a rosary and a turban of white cloth and received his blessing."

Shah Jahan, who substantially modified Jahangir's pavilion at Jahangirabad, went there to hunt soon after his accession to the throne. The sport delighted him with its abundance but he did not think the building "such as it should have been". He ordered a new building of exquisite design and beauty. On the Emperor's next visit Wazir Khan – who clearly knew how to impress – presented his majesty with a travelling throne of gold, 50 horses of Irak and "other curiosities valued at two lakhs". For his part his Majesty went off again to pay his respects to Saints Mian Mir and Sheikh Bilawal.

In 1631, while the Court was in session at Lahore, Ali Mardan Khan, Governor of Kandahar – a Persian possession for the previous 10 years – surrendered the city to the Emperor and then joined him in Lahore. Shah Jahan not surprisingly received him kindly and made him an Amir of the first rank. "The Khan, having paid his obeisance, offered his majesty a gift of one thousand gold pieces, and was honoured with a Khila'at, consisting of silk and embroidered clothes, a jewelled turban with aigrette, a jewelled dagger, shield and sword. He was created an Amir with the rank of 6,000 personnel, and received two horses with embroidered saddles and four elephants with silver housings, one of the elephants named Koh Shikan, being remarkable for its size." The enormous expenses of the trip from Kandahar were all paid by the State Treasury. "As he had come from a fertile and cool country, the Emperor was pleased to appoint him to the Governorship of Kashmir."

Lahore at this time was at the height of its splendour, and the people prosperous as never before. "Besides the countless military retainers of the Emperor, the picturesque cavalcades of the Princes Royal, and the attendants of the numerous nobles and Grandees of State, the sight of the Governors and Viceroys of provinces from the Narbada and Tapti to the confines of Kandahar and Gazni, and their vast hosts of followers, who came here to pay their homage to the Shahinshah (King of Kings) afforded a most imposing and gorgeous spectacle. Here came also the envoys of foreign nations, the bearers of friendly letters to the Emperor, or of the curiosities of their respective countries to present to him...On each visit to the mausoleum of his father the Emperor distributed not less than ten thousand rupees etc."

The former Governor of Kandahar rose rapidly. Later that same year he was created Viceroy of Lahore and Kashmir, with a rank of 7,000 personnel and 7,000 horses; and doubtless to show his appreciation received permission to entertain Shah Jahan with a Persian-style firework display in the Fort. The Emperor was delighted. The poor got another "rupees ten thousand".

Another report of largesse has a more modern ring. In 1634 excessive rains and flooding ruined the harvest. Thousands of needy peasants invaded Lahore for relief, and presented themselves to the Emperor at the public audience of the Jharoka. "The Emperor was pleased to grant a lakh of rupees for their relief, and it was ordered that as long as they stayed in the capital, food should be distributed to them daily. Fifty-thousand rupees were also sent to Kashmir for the relief of the famine-stricken."

Yet it all ended badly. As he aged, the Emperor's powers declined significantly and he rallied too late. Already his three younger sons were ranged against the Prince Regent – Darah Shikoh, the favourite of the Emperor – who stayed with his father in Agra.

Though furthest from the seat of power the third son, Aurangzeb had proved by far the ablest and in 1657 easily out-manoeuvred both his brothers and his father. Dara Shikoh took refuge in Lahore, where he was something of a darling to the inhabitants for the favour he had always shown the city and its people. He had built numerous beautiful buildings and market-places there and demonstrated a breadth and generosity of mind which reminded people of Akbar.

Despite popular support, however, the heir apparent lost the decisive battle fought against Aurangzeb's army in the plains of the Punjab. Shah Jahan had already been forced to surrender to Aurangzeb the Red Fort of Agra, and there he lived a prisoner, for the rest of his days.

Despite this sad decline, for creative energy, versatility and splendour of achievement Shah Jahan stands out beyond compare among Mughal builders. The Emperor Augustus of Rome is said to have boasted that he found that city brick and left it marble. It was of course an exaggeration, but with much truth in the claim.

Shah Jahan might have made a similar boast: that he was born into a world agreeable in red sandstone; and that he rebuilt it, magnificent, in marble.

FATAL ORNAMENT

The last of the great Mughals, who reigned longer than all his predecessors and heirs, and gave the city of Lahore the biggest mosque in the world, the Badshahi, was one of those fatal figures of history who dominated all the events and overshadowed all the other personalities of his age, yet failed to secure the future of his own house.

Probably the most impenetrable of all the Mughals, and by some the least liked and most feared, Aurangzeb (1618-1707) kept his father captive – in sight of the Taj he had built in memory of his wife – till he died. He murdered, among others, his older brother, the Prince Regent Dara Shikoh, and enforced the letter of the Sharia law with such severity that rebellion by the majority Hindu in Delhi was immediate and, though ruthlessly suppressed at the time, never thereafter wholly contained.

Happily, Lahore saw little of these troubles while Aurangzeb lived. The turbulence mounting elsewhere within the Empire passed the Seat of Empire by and the city continued in the security of good government provided by Aurangzeb who, though absent most of the time in the Deccan, remained watchful, kept himself fully briefed on events in all major centres, and acted decisively wherever remedy was required.

The first of the half-dozen visits Aurangzeb paid to Lahore was the year after his coronation. He stayed in the Faiz Bakhsh pavilion of the Shalamar Gardens. Together with his son Prince Mohamed Azim and provincial dignitaries he inspected the Fort and left detailed instructions for its upkeep. He also visited the Wazir Khan mosque and offered prayers. He declared Khalil-Ullah Khan Viceroy of Punjab in reward for services rendered, and made many other appointments. Then he left for Delhi.

In the course of the first two visits he paid the city in 1662, Aurangzeb ordered construction of his supreme Lahore legacy – the Badshahi Mosque. He had told the Friday congregation at the Firoz Khan mosque he attended that they must continue to assemble for ever on that spot to recite their prayers. It's commonly assumed that he was obeyed to the letter and that the now lost Firoz Khan building used to stand where the Badshahi Mosque was built.

This vast undertaking was among the last works of the Mughal period of architecture, and was probably inspired by the Jamia Mosques of Delhi and Agra which pre-date it. It's even more massive than they are.

Entirely constructed of brick, dressed with red limestone, and with white marble domes and ornament, the mosque forms a 170-metre square, elevated on a platform. Its main, eastern entry is up 22 formidable steps. Large tablets in Urdu and English relate the history of its building and note its official capacity of 60,000 people. Those who should know say it's actually more like 100,000.

That's no surprise when you've removed your shoes and had a glimpse inside the massive gate. This entrance is pure Mughal in style, with a central arch, tall and graceful. Its exterior walls are painstakingly decorated with sculptured panels and each corner is marked by a squared tower, topped by a red sandstone turret capped with a white marble cupola. This white-capped turret idea is repeated on a larger scale atop the 53-metre high minarets which mark the corners of the mosque. The view from the top of these is said to be very beautiful, as one can imagine: especially over the fort. Sher Singh, one of Ranjit Singh's sons, used these stately towers as cannon positions for shelling the fort in 1841.

The floor of the vast court was originally paved in brick laid in prayer carpet, *musallah*, shapes and bordered with black stone. The 80 cells, *hujras*, built into the walls were originally study rooms. The British demolished them in 1856. They were rebuilt to form arcades and some turned into halls for ablutions.

Opposite the entrance stands the Prayer Hall, on its 25 by 82-metre platform. With its red sandstone front, main, central archway and side arches, crenellated walls, minaret corners and magnificent white domes this hall, for all its relatively small size, is well proportioned and very fine.

Discreet white marble floral decoration relieves the otherwise unbroken red of the sandstone exterior, and inside there are eight arches of massive height, so designed to carry the enormous weight of the three glorious white marble domes on the roof. There are floral motifs in relief around the walls. The Mehrab and its corner stones are faced in marble.

From the Mosque you return to the Hazuri Bagh of Ranjit Singh. This square garden was originally the place where Aurangzeb reviewed his troops. The

other side of it is where the second major Lahore work of Aurangzeb confronts you: the Alamgiri Gate. The name is one of his titles and means "Conqueror of the Universe".

Aurangzeb built this to complete a realignment of the fort wall which would bring it parallel with the facade of the Badshahi Mosque. Its military character is inescapable. It's simply enormous, flanked by semi-circular fluted bastions and topped by towers with domes. It's the essence of military Mughal – and brings to mind the rueful complaint of one of Aurangzeb's battlefield adversaries: "To fight Aurangzeb is to fight one's own fate".

Aurangzeb's gate seems to share Fate's intransigence.

Shortly after Aurangzeb ordered the building of the Badshahi and left, Lahore was gravely threatened, and in parts actually damaged, by encroachments of the fickle river Ravi. Aurangzeb immediately sent instructions to build a brick embankment more than six kilometres long to protect the city. The bulwark was faced in lead. Steps down to the river were provided so that people could wash and bathe. There were also gardens along the entire length of the embankment, irrigated by Persian wheels worked by bullocks. (Part of this embankment was unearthed recently near the north-west wall of the Fort). The embankment is credited with saving Lahore and changing the course of the Ravi to a safer bed, two kilometres away to the north.

On another visit about this time a grand Darbar was held in the Shah Burj built by his father Shah Jahan. The building was described at the time as "the bestower of dignity on the highest heaven" and as "a house of wonders, in attempting to see which the sun, ascending the nine steps of heaven each morning, is exalted". There was a great display of splendour and magnificence. Aurangzeb, being then 46, was weighed against gold, silver and other metals which were then distributed among the poor.

Other Lahore monuments from Aurangzeb's time include the tiled mosque inside the Taxali Gate, built by one of Fidai Khan Koka's aides, Amir Abdullah Khan – who may also be responsible for another mosque which once stood in the *Nakhas Khana*, Horse Market, outside what is today called the Landa Bazaar, and another constructed in 1659 by the historian Mohamed Saleh Kamboh Lahori, inside the Mochi Gate. This mosque is well-known for its exquisite and colourful glazed tiles. His house, though much altered, is preserved inside the Mochi Gate. He himself is buried in a mausoleum now used as a church on the Bin Badis Road.

Also admired for the beauty of the glazed tiles on its exterior walls is another mosque inside the Mochi Gate, near Takiya Sadhuan. It was completed in 1671 by Afraz Khan.

Possibly from this time, though perhaps dating from the reign of Shah Jahan, is the unique tomb – built inside a tank and accessible only through a causeway – of the wife of Dara Shikoh, who died fleeing from Aurangzeb with her husband before treachery delivered him to execution.

Aurangzeb died in the Deccan in 1707, and was succeeded on the throne by his Lahore Governor, Prince Mohamed Muazzam. But the throne could not make the monarch.

The majesty and the mystique of the Mughals ended with Aurangzeb's death.

The results were especially serious for Lahore. No city had benefitted more from the creative patronage of the great Mughals. Now, neglected by the lesser men who succeeded to their throne, and – in consequence – increasingly ravaged by Sikh invaders the great centre of Mughal culture went into decline. A whole century was to pass before action was taken to halt it.

4 Pearl for Plunder

Abrupt change in Mughal fortunes followed Aurangzeb's death in 1707.

In the 182 years since the start of Babur's reign in 1525 there had been six Mughal Emperors. In the next 61 years there were 10!

The first two – Shah Alam Bahadur Shah (1707-1712) and Jahandar Shah (1712-1713) – fought their way to the throne from the ever strong office of Governor of Lahore.

Shah Alam Bahadur was a Shi'ite. While in Lahore to put down Sikh insurgents he inserted words in the *Kalima*, public confession of faith, which the majority Sunni congregation found unacceptable. They showed how they felt by cutting to pieces the preacher who had obeyed the Shah's decree. His majesty revoked his order.

Soon afterwards the Shah issued an order that all the city's dogs should be killed. He was easily defied. People hid their animals during that day and took them across the river next morning. He died aged 70 in 1712, popular with the people despite – or maybe because of – his foibles. They named a city gate after him.

Jahandar Shah moved his court to Delhi, but within a year a nephew deposed and murdered him. Thereafter none of the Mughal Emperors showed the slightest interest in Lahore. Their line dragged on for another 150 years but none so much as tried to visit the ancient bastion of their once great Empire.

Inevitably both suffered for the neglect. Persians and Afghans in particular quickly saw the isolation to which Lahore and the whole of wealthy Punjab was reduced, and in no time the Mughals were watching helplessly as the once secure bulwark of the north-west, with all its prodigious commercial wealth and incomparable cultural treasures, became the savage hunting ground of every kind of robber and plunderer.

The story of the next 150 years reminds one irresistibly of Sher Shah Suri's lament: he should have destroyed a prize too rich to be left in peace.

The reality of their situation was quickly grasped by the citizens of Lahore and their rulers. Effectively they started to govern themselves, without referring to Delhi; assumed, in fact, a kind of independence. They enjoyed the dedicated service of some gifted and single-minded leaders, like the Nawab Abdul Samad Khan who governed the city first in the name of Farrukh Sayir (Emperor in 1713) and then continued in charge through the next four reigns. One of the decisive moves made by the canny Nawab, to forestall the worst effects of the anarchy he foresaw, was to leave the citadel and shift his centre of operations to the enormously wealthy Lahore suburb of Mughal-pura.

Opposite: Fluted and gilded dome over tomb of the fifth Sikh guru, Arjun Dev, dates from the reign of Ranjit Singh (1799-1839).

This district already contained the tomb of the saintly Khawand Mahmood (d. 1643), the Gateway of the *Gulabi Bagh*, Rose Garden, built in 1655, the so-called mausoleum of Dai Anga, the tomb of Ali Mardan Khan (d. 1655) and his mother, and several others.

Now – in the area of the suburb called Begumpura after his wife (northeast of today's Railway Station) – the Nawab built his own fortress and, despite what was going on in the city centre, continued to add yet more sumptuous palaces, gardens, mosques, aqueducts, baths and taverns and a very popular bazaar. The Nawab then handed the office on to his son, and to his son's sons. From 1713 to 1748 the Vice-Royalty of Lahore became in effect "hereditary", giving the Punjab capital much greater stability than the Empire itself enjoyed.

Nevertheless with the covetous eyes of Sikhs, Marathas (a Hindu dynasty from the Deccan) and the Afghans of chief Durrani forever fixed on Punjab, even the bravest determination could not cope for ever. The proud province once again found itself prey to plunder, arson and wanton destruction.

With no outside backing or help Lahore wilted under the constant attacks, and at last, inevitably, Begumpura suffered. In 1746, when Durrani first attacked Lahore, one day's plunder of the suburb so satisfied his troops that they left Lahore itself untouched.

Later the Sikhs were to do even more damage: razing many of its buildings to the ground and building their own palaces with the marble and bricks. The devastation continued under the British, who saw the once fine suburb as nothing more than a quarry for the fine materials from which they might build public and private buildings of their own. Today only parts of the palaces, a few graves, a mausoleum and a couple of mosques remain: sufficient however to show the decline of Mughal architecture which was occurring in these later years.

Some of these battles around Lahore were so bloody that the scene of one engagement – at Mahmud Buti in 1752 – was still covered with human bones more than a hundred years later. Already before then the King of Persia, Nadir Shah in 1739 had sacked and pillaged the poor city and Ahmad Shah Durrani – the Afghan chief – did so repeatedly. Both used Lahore as a base for their various attempts on the Delhi throne.

In 1759 the vicious circle of despotism was finally completed when Ahmad Shah Abdali took the Punjab back into his Afghan Empire. But in 1768 he again abandoned the city and the Sikhs wasted no time settling ancient scores with their former Muslim overlords. "The Rule of the Sikhs" – it was said – "was the Rule of Lawlessness".

The Sikhs ruled Lahore from 1768 to 1849. The end of Muslim rule in the province and its once glorious capital, Lahore, was made final in 1768 with its surrender to a Sikh Triumvirate of Gujjar, Lahna and Sobha Singh. The first held the area from the Shalamar Gardens to the city – where he built a fort in his own name; the second had the Fort and various of the old city gates; Sobha Singh was charged with the area now called Nawankot. The Afghan Ahmad Shah Durrani went on trying to oust the Sikhs, but he ended up bowing to reality and confirmed Lahna Singh as "his" *de facto* governor.

Opposite: Samadhi of Ranjit Singh, built at the place of his cremation. Uncontested master of the region through four decades of the 19th century, Ranjit Singh, though illiterate, showed great intellectual curiosity. He surrounded himself with both Muslim and Hindu counsellors.

From 1799 to 1839 the Sikh chieftain Ranjit Singh provided a period of continuity which for the now grievously suffering Mughal city had two grim advantages: he kept the British at bay till after he died in 1839 and the troublesome Afghans west of the Khyber Pass for a like period.

Ranjit Singh however lacked successors of his calibre. In the 10 years after his death his seven sons allowed their power to dissipate to a point where in 1849 the British – having concluded one Treaty of Lahore recognising the Sikh

Maharajah, but seeing him unable to deliver the loyalty of many of his troops – simply annexed the Punjab. Their first Governor-General, Dalhousie, granted the Maharajah Dalip Singh a pension and off he went to live in exile in England.

These political events were background to a horrible trauma. What happened to Lahore under the Sikhs and during the first 50 years of the British Raj makes dire reading. Today's visitor to this great city need not dwell on what has been lost; but nearly a century of destruction cannot be ignored. The following summary is taken from a manuscript of Dr Saifur Rahman Dar. Taking their revenge for past grievances, Dr Dar says:

Opposite: Interior of the Samadhi of Ranjit Singh. The pavilion is inlaid with pietra dura. The marble urn contains the Maharajah's ashes. The other urns hold the ashes of four queens and seven slave girls who immolated themselves on his pyre.

"The Sikhs put the sacred monuments of Muslims to profane use and turned their mosques and mausoleums into stables, stores for gun-powder and private residences. They disfigured the symmetrically laid out Mughal Palaces, big residential buildings called havelis and gardens, by hotch-potch additions and super-impositions like the one still standing on top of Shish Mahal in the Lahore Fort and a pavilion on the first terrace of Shalamar Gardens. Above all, they built their own palatial houses and sacred structures from the spoils of Muslim monuments in the city. They denuded the sparkling Mughal buildings of all their embellishments to be used clumsily in their own buildings. There is hardly any major or minor historical building in the city which was spared. The grand Badshahi Mosque was used as a military cantonment and during internecine wars heavy cannons were mounted on top of its lofty minarets for bombarding inside the fort. When Maharajah Ranjit Singh died in 1839 his samadhi or mausoleum – a building in a semi-Islamic style – was erected very awkwardly just in front of the Roshanai gate thus barring its use as a gate. The Golden Mosque was occupied by the Sikhs and the Holy Sikh book – 'Granth' – was placed inside it. The Mausoleum of Jahangir was denuded of its marble veneering, particularly its pavilion on the roof, before it was allowed to be used as residence by Sardar Sultan Mahmood Khan of Kabul, who burnt fire in its halls. The magnificent garden was turned into a jungle. The worst sufferers among the monuments of Lahore were the tombs of Asaf Khan and of his sister Queen Nur Jahan. The marble slabs from the pear-shaped dome of the former were ruthlessly removed down to the last piece. William Moorcraft, a traveller, himself saw these slabs being removed and even trees in the garden were sold. The same happened with the red-stone and cloud-colour (Sang-i-Abri) stone of the mausoleum of Nur Jahan. Even her and her daughter's graves in the subterranean chamber were opened in search of treasures, desecrated and their bones thrown into the river Ravi. The magnificent tomb of Anarkali was converted into the residence of Kharrak Singh, the crown Prince. Shah Chiragh Mosque and Begum Shahi Mosque were converted into magazines for gun-powder. The palatial haveli of Wazir Khan called Pari Mahal was systematically denuded of its valuable stones and converted into a powder-magazine. Of this building complex now only a small mosque is extant. The Hospice of Shah Bilawal near Kot Khawaja Saeed was converted into a hunting ground with a pavilion called Baradari Sher Singh. Similarly, the gateway of the Mausoleum of Ali Mardan Khan was used as residence by one Gurdat Singh, an officer of Ranjit's army, whereas the mausoleum proper was converted into a powder-magazine. Beautiful slabs of red and yellow sand-stone were also removed from the mausoleum. The Mosque of Dai Anga was also used as a magazine for gun-powder during the Sikh regime. Within the Fort itself, the Sikhs converted the Pearl Mosque into Pearl Temple (Moti Mandir) and made awkward additions and alterations in the Shish Mahal area.

Above: Lion of the Punjab, the ruler Ranjit Singh.

The most prestigious area of Lahore during the 19th Century was Begumpura. First, it was looted by Ahmad Shah Abdali. Then, three times it was plundered during the Triumvirate rule; and final destruction fell on it during Ranjit Singh's reign when all of its significant buildings were dug up – down to the foundations – in search of bricks to be used for building hundreds of their own palatial buildings. All the marble from the family graveyard of Nawab Zakriya Khan was removed by Ranjit Singh himself. Shalamar gardens was first plundered by the three Sikh Rulers who removed precious stones worth lakhs of rupees. A single tank of jade is said to have been sold for 25,000 rupees. Later on, Ranjit Singh himself removed the entire marble and red sand-stone used in four pavilions, and fountains in the tanks, and canals and marble trellis work and sent the lot to Amritsar. The mausoleum of Nawab Mian Khan, son of Nawab Saadullah Khan in Bhogiwal village was first used as a residence of Raja Sochet Singh and then stripped of all its valuable stone veneers etc etc. The so-called Nawan Kot area had a Mughal garden and a mausoleum, now wrongly attributed to Zebun Nisa Begum, daughter of Aurangzeb. One of the Triumvirate rulers, Sobha Singh made this mausoleum-garden his headquarters. He spoiled the entire garden, its pathways and fountains. Even the neighbouring mausoleum of Rustam Ghazi – the patron saint of Princess Zebun Nisa was not spared. It is said that the entire marble used in Hazuri Bagh pavilion was taken from the so-called mausoleum of Zebun Nisa which now stands in stark nudity – a protest against Sikh vandalism – and that the pavilion on the roof of Jahangir's mausoleum was bodily removed and reconstructed here. Haveli Mian Khan inside Mochi Gate, entirely built of black marble, was converted into a factory for making gun-powder. When the powder exploded the entire palace was destroyed."

These depredations by the Sikhs, like those of the British later, were generally associated with the notion of contributing some architectural splendour of their own to Lahore. With no solid tradition of their own in the area it was natural that the Sikhs should imitate to a great extent the domes, arches, pillars and vaultings used by the great Mughal architects.

The Badshahi Mosque of the latter, and the Samadhi of Ranjit Singh built adjacent to it, illustrate this and make it possible to compare the two achievements. Pretty in pink, and bubbling with minarets, the Samadhi is one of the most eye-catching features this side of old Lahore. Together with the Samadhi of Guru Arjan Dev it is considered among the best Sikh monuments in the city.

The massive northern fortification wall of the fort is also Sikh – constructed by Ranjit Singh after the river had shifted north-west. The Sikhs also built numerous *havelis*, mansions, several of which – including the *havelis* of Kallu Bai Ahluwalia inside Yaki gates, of Dhayan Singh in the Hira Mandi area, of the Jamadar Kushal Singh near the Fort, deserve mention. They are vast, and many of them today used as Government offices.

The *haveli* Kanwar Nau Nihal Singh still retains beautiful frescos – though these are now at grave risk for lack of proper upkeep. The Sikhs also constructed numerous gardens (Baghs), but with the exception of the Bagh and mausoleum of Rani Gulbadan in the Miani area, all have been lost.

The British rule ran virtually a hundred years – from 1849-1947.

When the Railway line from Multan to Lahore was being laid in the second half of Queen Victoria's 19th century the contractor was allowed by the British to use the 4,500-year-old burnt bricks of Harappa – an ancient city of the Punjab, and one of the principal centres of the Indus Valley civilisation that flourished from 2500 to 1700BC – as ballast for 80 kilometres of track. The

damage thus done to this sister city of Mohenjo-Daro is both indescribable and irreparable. (For the sake of the marble the British are also said to have put the Taj Mahal up for auction: though happily the contractor decided that the cost of quarrying the world's most universally admired building was greater than the marble was worth…).

Consciously or unconsciously, during the first half of their 98 years of rule, the British seem to have done all they could to separate Lahore from her glorious Mughal past. Mausolea, mosques, hospices: none was spared. Royal apartments in the Fort were pulled down to make way for barracks, and until Lord Curzon took things in hand at the turn of the century and reversed such measures the lovely Pearl Mosque was used as a Treasury. Underground halls in the glorious Shish Mahal were converted into wine-cellars; and its Hall of Common Audience, *Diwan-i-Aam*, together with the Royal Baths, taken for a hospital. Soldiers used the *Diwan-i-Khas*, Hall of Private Audience, as a Church. Shah Jahan's *Khawabgah*, sleeping-quarters, were used for military offices.

In 1856 they restored the Badshahi Mosque to its original function but first pulled down the 80 study cells which used to surround the great court and erected the arcades now seen in their place.

The so-called "Anarkali's Tomb," used as a Lord's residence during the Sikh period, now became a Protestant church. The grave was dug up and the cenotaph pushed aside. (The Punjab Record office and Archive Museum is now housed in it).

The beautiful serai adjacent to Jahangir's mausoleum was used as a railway works depot and at one time was considered a likely site for Lahore's first Railway Station…

Above: Lahore's main railway station. Establishment of the railway system by the British provided an invaluable means of communication, but at the heavy cost of laying waste vast areas of the old city, with all their mosques, palaces, gardens and other monuments.

*Opposite: Chandeliers light
the interior of the Quaid-i-
Azam library.*

*Above: Increasingly concerned
for the glories of the past,
authorities are lavishing care
and money on restoring the
ancient building which houses
Lahore's main post office.*

The Railway in fact did Muslim monuments more harm than any other single interest. All the ancient localities between Badami Bagh and today's Mughalpura Railway Station were levelled to make way for it. Many ancient and fine mosques were sacrificed, together with the Dara Shikoh bazaar. Bahadur Khan's lofty mausoleum became a dance-hall. The mausoleum of Nawab Nusrattullah Khan was absorbed into the Railway Buildings and is today a railway office. The magnificent Dai Anga mosque – now next to Platform 1! – had already been used by Ranjit Singh for storing gunpowder. Under the British it became a railway manager's residence.

It is still not clear whether the dismantling of the city's nine metre high wall and the infilling of the moat was carried out to demilitarise the city or for reasons of hygiene. Either way it deprived Lahore of one of its most significant landmarks.

In justice, there were many positive sides to British rule. They attended to matters of public health, education, and medical care.

Under Lord Curzon, and since, a serious effort was made by the British authorities to compensate for earlier ravages through restoration of Lahore

Fort, the Shalamar Gardens, Jahangir's Mausoleum and Ali Mardan Khan's: *Above: Interior of Islamia* the loftiest monument in the city. He secured passage of a law for the *College.* preservation of old monuments and set up a Department of Government specifically to oversee this.

But already before Curzon the British had begun their own substantial and original contribution to Lahore's architectural heritage. In a remarkably successful hybrid style, improbably and inelegantly, yet succintly, described as "Mughal-Victorian" they erected numerous grand public and private buildings which, where they have been preserved, add an invaluable dimension to the city's rich architectural range and interest.

Outstanding examples border, or lie within easy reach of the Shahrah-i-Quaid-i-Azam main artery (The Mall) of the city. They include the many fine colleges and schools which found Lahore's reputation as education centre of Pakistan *par excellence*. Most notable are Government College – first in prestige in the country, and of which Allama Muhamad Iqbal, founding father of Pakistan's Independence, was a distinguished alumnus; the Foreman Christian College, founded in 1864 in rented rooms near the Shah Almi Gate

by an American missionary and transferred to its present campus in 1940, originally in two blocks but now, in 180 acres, expanded to five student hostels and with its own mosque, added in 1950; the Kinnaird College for Women, the Islamia College – prominent in the campaign for Independence and another institution where Iqbal was active; and Aitcheson (Chiefs) College, still the most expensive educational establishment in the country.

The fortlike Railway Station – object at the time of much discontent for the ravages its system inflicted upon venerable reaches of the ancient city – was started in 1859 under Sir John Lawrence, Chief Commissioner for the Punjab (1858-1859). (The Railway remains, incidentally, the largest landowner in the

city.) The pure Doric hall built to commemorate Lawrence's services – together with that erected in honour of the first Lieutenant-Governor, Sir Robert Montgomery (1859-1863) now form the finest library in Pakistan, the Quaid-i-Azam. The structures were superb and they are superbly maintained. The old Lawrence Gardens, begun in 1860 with 112 acres, and subsequently enlarged, are the biggest in the city. Adjacent is the country's biggest zoo.

In 1870 what is now the country's largest medical institution of its kind, the King Edward Medical College, started life, named – for the British Viceroy to India assassinated in 1872 – the Mayo Hospital and Medical School.

Also named after this Lord Mayo when it was founded was today's National College of Arts. Its first principal was a teacher of painting and sculpture from Bombay: Lockwood, father of Rudyard Kipling. His charge of the Arts School was combined with responsibilities as Curator of the Lahore Museum. When the local market became flooded with inferior goods from Britain, Kipling's School became a haven for the finest Lahore craftsmen in weaving, cotton printing, wood-carving and other skills. By 1915 there were 28 industrial schools in the Punjab under the School's standard. Today the National College runs separate departments in Architecture, Fine Arts and Design, and on a competition entry basis receives 450 students from all over the country.

About the same time as the Arts School, the oldest University in Pakistan opened its doors in Lahore in 1882 as the Punjab University. Its main buildings are now further south but the original structure, in pure Islamic style, still stands on the Shahrah-i-Quaid-i-Azam (Mall), almost opposite the Museum.

The nucleus of Lahore Museum's outstanding collection was put together in the middle of the 19th century and housed in the Wazir Khan pavilion

Right: Lahore Museum, oldest
and largest in Pakistan, was
inaugurated in 1894 by Prince
Victor Albert to mark Queen
Victoria's Golden Jubilee. Its
seventeen galleries cover the
full spectrum of the history and
culture of Pakistan and
neighbouring regions.

before it was shifted in 1864, to what is now Tollinton Market. Its imposing, new, permanent home was completed in 1892 and has remained a city landmark ever since.

The coins, paintings and sculptures are outstanding. The coins – 50,000 of them going back to the 6th century B.C. – include the best Indo-Greek examples ever produced anywhere on the sub-continent, both for inscription and impression. And – of special importance to the student of coins – the whole collection is published and available.

The paintings number about two thousand, and the most important section

Below: The famous Fasting Buddha, considered the supreme masterpiece of Lahore Museum's many galleries. Like other superb carvings from the Gandhara civilizations whose cradle was Taxila – thirty-five kilometres north of modern Rawalpindi – the sculpture is a powerful fusion of Buddhist, eastern elements, Greek and western influences. Other famous pieces exhibited in Lahore Museum include the miracle of Srasvati and the Greek Goddess Athena.

Below: Another example of the strength and nobility of Gandhara sculptures. The art flourished from the 1st to the 5th centuries.

105

Above: Lahore Cathedral. The cross formerly surmounted the dome of the so-called Tomb of Anarkali, which was consecrated as the church of St. James on 24 June 1857. It was moved to its present site when the current Cathedral was built in 1927.

Right: Zamzama stands large on an island in the middle of the road outside Lahore Museum. The 18th century gun was immortalised as 'Kim's Gun' by Rudyard Kipling.

comes from the Punjab Hill Schools, with Hindu religious themes. This is the earliest and best-known such collection, with an abundance of quality, and proven, originals.

In the Gandhara room the remarkable exhibition of Greco-Buddhist art is dominated by the famous, unique, fasting Buddha. The unlikely marriage of western (Greek) with Asian (Buddhist) artistic tradition produced many

masterpieces displayed here.

Outside the museum, not far away, Zamzama, the 18th century firepiece immortalised by Kipling as 'Kim's Gun', takes up a surprising length of space in the middle of the road.

Nearby too are the General Post Office – which started life in 1880 as the *Kothi Tar Ghar*, Telegraph Office, when this means of communication was introduced to the country – and the stately High Court. Other notable buildings from the British period include the magnificent Town Hall and the Free Masonic Lodge; the latter preserved, thanks to the efforts of a dedicated conservationist lobby, and now being turned into a Museum for Punjab Arts and Crafts.

These foreign contributions to Lahore's inventory of treasures are a tribute both to the builders and to the spirit of the land they occupied. For the former had great and ancient building traditions of their own, but in Lahore they bowed to the excellence of the Islamic, Mughal inspiration and were themselves powerfully inspired by it. It was this same sturdy Islamic spirit which in the 20th century was to carry the Muslim people to Independence. And – as ever in the history of Islam in the sub-continent – Lahore was again to play a leading role in the achievement.

Above: Elegant lines of Lawrence Montgomery Hall which is now Lahore's Quaid-i-Azam library.

5 Lest thy Little Dust...

Before the entrance to the Badshahi Mosque, guarded by soldiers in dress uniform – red on grey – stands to one side in quiet dignity the tomb of one of Pakistan's founding fathers. Allama Muhammad Iqbal – scholar, poet, and statesman – was born in neighbouring Sialkot, but lived most of his life in Lahore.

Iqbal did not live to see the Muslim community achieve the national independence of which he was the most eloquent early protagonist. But it was his presidential address to the All-India Muslim League at Allahabad in 1930 which set out the most lucid exposition of the argument that for the healthy development of Islam in South Asia it was essential to have a separate Muslim state at least in the sub-continent's north-west. Subsequent correspondence with Quaid-i-Azam Mohammed Ali Jinnah added the Muslim north-east.

Three years later students gave the name Pakistan to the proposed state, but even then, very few, even among Muslims, welcomed Iqbal's bold proposal. It was to take another decade, and the dynamic leadership of the Quaid, before the demand for a separate state would be widely approved.

In 1940, two years after Iqbal died, the League, meeting in Lahore, formulated its now famous "Pakistan Demand" for a separate Muslim homeland in Muslim majority regions of the subcontinent.

The Minar-i-Pakistan – the single most outstanding modern monument in Lahore – immortalises the passage of this resolution, and the date: 23 March 1940.

At length after much turmoil on August 14th, 1947, the newly carved out West Punjab came into being under the newly independent flag of Pakistan. Its capital: Lahore.

In the forty years since then the young country has seen its share of problems, including civil unrest resulting in martial law, three major wars with its neighbour, the loss of its Eastern province – now Bangladesh – and most recently the influx of more than three-million refugees from Afghanistan, who greatly inflated the numbers of homeless who had already poured in from East Punjab and further east.

In 1955 for good measure the river Ravi again burst its banks. It caused immense hardship to an estimated two-million people.

And yet, throughout these tumultuous decades Lahore has gone on growing, thriving on the spirit which brought the city unbowed through so many previous harsh twists of fate.

For this city which Sher Shah Suri would have razed to the ground is no museum piece. It is almost frighteningly vital. You don't have to go there to recognise this. At Independence in 1947 it counted a population of half a million. By the mid '80's that figure had ballooned to four-million. A fifth million will be added before the century ends.

Opposite: Provincial Assembly Hall – seat of the Punjab Provincial Government. Lahore is capital of this most populous of the country's provinces.

Physically the city has expanded beyond recognition, and the ancient centre from which everything else sprang is now, by comparison, surprisingly small.

The growth is in every direction but above all to the south, where the Government-sponsored housing schemes and shopping centres, University and Research establishments, industrial engineering plants and other facilities are creating, effectively, a New Lahore.

And yet, for all this challenging new lease on life, Lahore consciously holds on to its past.

And since, as Dr Dar has said: "For all practical purposes the history of Lahore is the history of the Mughals in Lahore," it's no wonder that the emphasis for the city's Development Authority has been directed lately towards living conditions in the ancient walled city.

Population expansion here – as in other cities – has led to fragmentation of large property units, increased traffic and consequent aggravation of the pressure on basic services like water supply, sewerage, waste disposal, and recreational facilities.

One of the earliest responses to growing demand for remedial action was unfortunately a reckless pulling down of older buildings and their replacement by featureless modern structures. "The limited open spaces," writes Dr Dar, "are also being encroached upon and built over."

In 1969/70 city authorities carried out an extensive survey and drew up a master plan of "Strategies for Upgrading, Renewal and Conservation." For lack of funding, however, nothing came of it.

Then in 1986 funds were guaranteed by the World Bank. The scheme was revived, and a new Conservation Plan for the Walled City commissioned. It aims to identify all "buildings and elements of historical significance and to establish their historical and cultural context." The next step will be to list in detail all the sites marked out for conservation: streets, buildings, open spaces, monuments and the like.

The Government meanwhile has identified certain areas for clearance and the development of water and power supplies, waste disposal, communications and fire prevention measures. In addition, a new Inner Circle road will be built – immediately outside the Walled City area with parklands established between it and the already existing Circular Road. This should improve traffic flow along the old city wall limits, besides providing relaxation amenities for residents of the ancient city area.

One of the grandest buildings in the old quarter – the Haveli Jamadar Khush-hal Singh, also known as the Haveli Dhayan Singh – has also been converted into a school – City College for Girls – the first such development inside the old Walled area.

Nonetheless there is a clear feeling that the Federal Department of Archaeology might have done more to preserve the common heritage by using better equipment and more trained technical experts. The Chief Minister of the Punjab was one who complained. The amount of money allocated is not to blame. In 1986 the funding for Lahore Fort alone was 1.5 million rupees. Control – it is believed – should henceforth be tripartite:

federal, provincial and at the Lahore area level.

Concerned residents and visitors alike would certainly rejoice at any measure that restores the city's manifest splendours to a condition closer to their original glory.

In fact relatively tiny volunteer groups like the Lahore Conservation Society have shown themselves remarkably successful in lobbying, for example, for restoration of the Free Masonic Lodge. A Museum of Punjab Folk Arts and Crafts is being prepared and upon completion will be housed here.

The Society stresses the need to protect and restore the non-Mughal heritage equally with the Muslim. Viewpoint Editor Mr Rahman points out that regardless of origin – Hindu, Muslim, Sikh or British – fine architecture is all part of Lahore's rich inheritance and should all be preserved. He draws particular attention to the surviving *havelis*. These rise in value all the time – simply as property – and their owners are unfortunately, therefore, less inclined to preserve as museum pieces residences of such obvious development potential.

The poise and charm that come from Lahore's felt continuity with its lively, varied past immediately strikes the visitor coming into the centre from the

Above: The Water and Power Development Authority (WAPDA) building continues the tradition of stylish building which has characterized Lahore for centuries. In the foreground are the Summit Minar and a superb marble pavilion, housing an open Qu'ran. Once it sheltered a statue of Queen Victoria – now in Lahore Museum.

Overleaf: Bikes, motor-bikes, motor-scooters, tongas, cars, carts, vans, buses, pedestrians, sheep, market stalls, trees, tall houses – and noise.

111

Opposite: The colour range of silks for sale in the bazaars continues the tradition of centuries in these unique emporia.

Below: In Lahore's old town happiness is a hookah.

Opposite: Betel-nut street, Lahore: heart of Pakistan's thriving film industry – although the horses aren't impressed.

115

Above: Confections made on the premises are sweet enough to tempt the most determined weight-watcher.

Right: Fast food in Lahore has nothing to do with multi-national food distribution chains or impersonal service. It's hot, fresh – and ever-ready.

airport via those wide and airy boulevard-like avenues with their broad sidewalks shaded by frequent trees, pleasing with lawns, flower beds and – especially along *Shahrah-i-Quaid-i-Azam*, the Mall – mansions and colleges, like Aitchison and Governor's House, in their superb garden settings.

Above: Bazaars showcase the work of highly-skilled craftsmen, who still work on the spot.

Gardens in fact remain a principal delight in this Mughal city of Gardens. Several new ones have been added since Independence: Jallu, Gulshan-i-Iqbal, Iqbal Park around the Minar-i-Pakistan, Model Town park, Race Course Park, and others, which deservedly attract not only town-dwellers but visitors from other cities as well. A gigantic Lahore Park on Rainwind Road is now proposed.

Sports lovers have three stadiums – including the country's biggest, Qaddafi Stadium, one of the arenas for the 1987 World Cup cricket finals, and a Sports Complex in Allama Iqbal (old Minto) Park. A Sports Museum is being set up in Olympic House.

Lahore's annual Horse and Cattle Show is of course famous. Here, in carnival atmosphere, the city's ancient past is vividly portrayed by the disciplined ranks of soldiers, the farmers showing off cattle and produce; the antics of performing animals; the tilt and thrust of the Mughal sport of polo. In recent years, the show has become the premier social event of the entire Punjab, anchoring Lahore's 1,000 year title as capital of the five-river province.

Endowed with the country's best colleges and schools, the only National Arts Centre, and the most museums in the country – including the oldest, the "Lahore", with its internationally famous exhibits, two Fine Arts Museums (Shakir Ali and Chugatai Trust – the only ones of their kind in Pakistan), the Faqir Khana and the National Museum of Science and Technology – it's hardly surprising that this Pearl of the Punjab easily maintains its place as cultural capital of this culturally rich land.

Opposite: Fresh fruit stall
recalls Lahore's traditional
source of wealth: the good
earth of the Punjab, constantly
renewed by the waters of its
five great rivers.

Below: Typical Lahori
enterpriser dries old bits of
cloth after washing them in a
pool and then sells them.

Opposite: In Lahore business
can be combined with
pleasure: a barber enjoys his
hookah while attending to
client.

Above: Room where Allama Muhammad Iqbal died on 21 April 1938. His house is now a museum commemorating his life-work.

Lahore has the largest concentration of college level graduates and the highest literacy rate in Pakistan. As citizens of a centre where so many civilisations have coalesced and so many influences been absorbed its people have acquired a well-deserved reputation for open-mindedness and readiness to entertain new ideas. To some it has seemed like political apathy! Lahore has seen it all before; it's difficult to get too excited about changes. Yet the fact is Lahore, its people and its rulers have played a decisive role in the affairs of the whole sub-continent – especially under the Mughals and more recently in achieving Independence.

Internationally too: Lahore had the distinction of hosting the first-ever International Islamic Colloquium – in December 1957 – and on the same occasion, in the Fort, the only international Exhibition of Islamic Arts ever held. In 1974 the city hosted the Second Conference of Heads of Islamic States – commemorated the following year by the Summit Minar.

Of modern buildings probably the finest is WAPDA HOUSE, headquarters of the Water and Power Development Authority – in chaste white and with the lines of a wide and lofty pagoda. Behind is the Punjab Assembly Hall and,

before both, the modern Summit Minar. Beside that, under a marble canopy where once, in stone, Queen Victoria sat enthroned, a Qu'ran lies open for reverent consultation by passers-by.

The City Arts Council's Al-Hamra complex is close by. In the tapering of its walls this excellent, modern, red-brick structure is reminiscent of the tomb of the famous saint Shah Rukn-i-Alam in Multan. But whereas pilgrims there walk around the shrine pausing to touch the venerable walls and pray, here they come to enjoy splendid productions staged in the two theatres, or to walk and admire the exhibitions of visual art handsomely displayed in the adjacent halls. A third hall called Music Centre is being added. The complex is unique in Pakistan.

Lahore has also recently emerged as headquarters of the country's thriving cinema industry, with virtually all the country's films now made here.

The city's love of celluloid fantasy and romance is easily seen in the numerous Picture Palaces and the huge crowds that attend them; while the energy of the industry's salesmen is equally evident from a walk along their highway – Betel Nut Street.

Above: Tomb of Allama Muhammad Iqbal, most articulate of the early champions of independence for Muslim India. It occupies a place of honour close to the entrance of the Badshahi Mosque.

There, the unfortunate old fortune-teller whose somnolent parrot reluctantly picks you the card that will reveal all, simply cannot compete with the forthcoming attractions of the big screen which the bills, posters and massive, screaming, hoardings luridly proclaim in such shocking colours you can't help feeling they really must frighten the horses...

In theatre, likewise, Lahore is the country's leader – not only in the Al Hamra complex but in Bagh-i-Jinna Open-Air stage productions and other settings which have proved popular with adult *cognoscenti* and family audiences alike.

Lahore is also noted for its fairs: so many of them that visitors from outlying hamlets, unwilling to go back home, are said to have inspired a saying: "In Lahore there are eight fairs in a week of seven days. I shall go back to my village once I have seen them all."

Most popular in all Punjab is the Fair of Lamps, while *Basant* – the Fair of Kites – is perhaps the most unusual and interesting. With their attendant fair-ground atmosphere, markets, circuses, and old-style theatre in mausoleum precincts these festivals and others create about Lahore a special feeling that life here is to be enjoyed.

Lahore, everyone says, is special.

So is its traffic! Wherever encountered the impression is indelible: an amazing Babel of blaring klaxons, horns and sirens, snarling Vespa motors and tearing tyres. It starts mornings before 6 and can still be in full-throated roar at midnight.

Traffic policemen at major intersections punctuate the discord with shrill

Left: Groom is garlanded with small fortune in currency notes for his wedding.

blasts of their whistles, and are heeded not for their noise – which is puny in the cacophony – but for their authority. Vehicles of all sizes, straining-at-the-leash for a contest from which they seem unfairly, momentarily, excluded, painfully bite back their impatience while bikes carrying two, three, even five passengers apiece manoeuvre for position at the ready – the Vespa drivers especially keen-eyeing each other and the field, nervous they might miss the minimalest advantage – till authority at length turns and, as if with a flag, launches all into the next lap.

To get the real feel of it, all you have to do is go for a ride in a motorised rickshaw – the Lahore "equivalent" of the tame taxi elsewhere. The experience has the unreality of a 3-D helter-skelter ride in a cinema. You sit on the

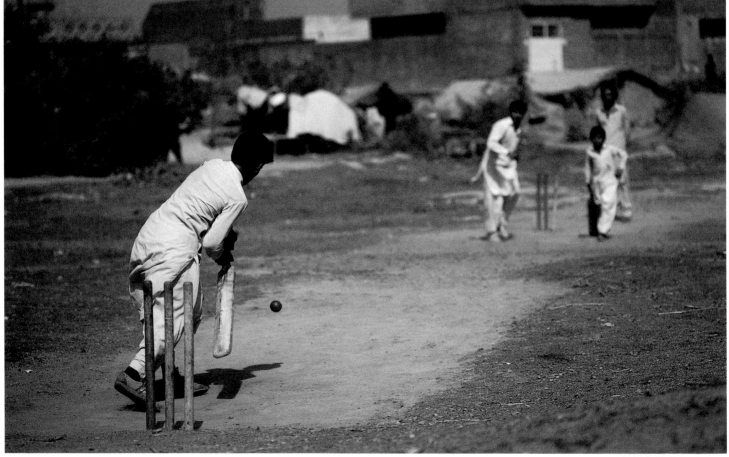

124

Opposite: Test-class Pakistani cricketers prepare for gruelling three-day first class match in Lahore's modern 40,000 seat arena – venue for the 1987 World Cup cricket tournament.

Pakistan's world squash champion Jahangir Khan practises at a Lahore court.

Opposite: Like squash and hockey, cricket is a national passion. Youngsters learn their skills early on strips marked out on waste ground.

Opposite: Beauty and the beasts – in the lion's den of a Lahore circus.

Above: Circus side-shows are never lost for novel ideas.

Opposite: Greater familiarity with elephants takes nothing away from the fun of feeding one at the Lucky Irani Circus of Pakistan, the country's biggest carnival.

much earthier: for here women – many of them wonderfully pretty, and all in gaily coloured dresses – collect dung of the buffalo brought here to wallow in the relative cool of a fetid pool. Using their hands the women transfer the dung to baskets which they carry on their cloth-covered heads to where it is dried for fuel.

Above: Cascading waters of man-made falls delight leisure lovers in Gulshan-i-Iqbal gardens.

One step up the ladder of toil other women wash salvaged old cloths in the same pool, dry them, and sell them as "remnants." Screen-makers – obviously successful at the top end of the local labour scale – supply the area's main industry.

But what is most striking at Shah Dara, apart from all the energy expended, is the good cheer: even of those with the meanest occupations. A scene which one might expect to leave with pity, one leaves admiring character.

Perhaps nowhere is Lahore's multi-coloured vitality more spectacular, though, than in the old city: at one of the ancient city entrances, for example, like the Delhi Gate. Bullocks, bikes, rickshaws, labouring buses, cars, scooters, elaborately decked and decorated coaches and lorries, horse-drawn carts, with uniformed schoolboys or demure young ladies aboard – the dignity of both seeming somehow to insulate them from the real world

Above: Tent-pegging contest at annual Horse and Cattle Show.

Right: Animals don't fly yet, but camels do dance at the National Horse and Cattle Show.

Above: Dancing dervishes provide fitting climax to Pakistan's most awaited event, the National Horse and Cattle Show.

Left: Waltz time for a fine Arabian horse at the National Horse and Cattle Show.

through which they are passing – converge where other cars, scooters,
bullocks and trucks are issuing through a gate Akbar founded four centuries
ago. Exactly where they meet a mosque has been sited: right in the way. It
forces the stew of vehicles into a spontaneous, live carousel more varied and
vivid than any fairground can show, through which pedestrians thread their
nervous ways to and from the security of the central mosque island, on the
skirts of which men wearing in their faces the buried lines of hard, open-air
living – and obviously unimpressed by the maelstrom of traffic about them –

squat for a shave, or to have their ears cleaned, to smoke a hookah, or just to squat!

Right by Delhi Gate younger men have commandeered an extravagant area of roadway for cleaning the outsides and interfering with the insides of a variety of other densely-packed vehicles. Beyond them, in a tradition as old as civilisation, families spread the wealth of garden, orchard and river produce on the ground and on stalls, inviting, like an endless walk-through stage set.

It's a non-stop performance, with noise so much part of the scene that, especially near the Gate, you don't realise its height, depth and breadth till you speak; and hear nothing!

The contrast with Lahore's almost polished new suburbs, and their often swanky new houses and tree-shaded ways, is about as great as you could expect to find in any one city. Yet it is all part of today's Lahore, and integral to it.

And the source of that unity is never far away. Visit the countless mosques and see – even against a background of old city noise – the deep recollection of old folk at prayer and younger ones receiving instruction. Sense the everywhere calm. Here, whatever your own religion, you may be sure you are at the taproot of both the vigorous, abundant growth, and the continuity with the past, which characterize today's Lahore.

An impression of green, flashing past the window before the aircraft thuds down onto Lahore's tarmac, separates into orchards, vegetables between rows of trees, grasses. The fertility of the Punjab may no longer be all that it once was, but – especially if you've flown straight from the desert browns around Karachi – the green still strikes you: much as it did envious outsiders in centuries past, luring them down from their barren mountains to maraud.

The terrain is, of course, still flat. No natural obstacles. No obvious protection. Not a mound to be seen in this land of mountains. So, you recognise Lahore's ancient vulnerability.

And if your timetable happily brings you to arrive early one evening in Spring: how agreeable the air as you step from the aircraft! Warm, yet light. Simply breathing pleases! You understand why the Mughals preferred Lahore to Delhi's oppressive heat and why the greatest of them lavished their greatest love and attention on this, their Seat of Empire.

Lahore today is at one with its past.

An exhibition at the British Museum in London dedicated to the works of Allama Muhammad Iqbal featured thoughts he penned to practise the calligraphy of which he was a master. One was translated:

> *Keep desire alive in thy heart*
> *Lest thy little dust become a tomb.*

Perhaps he addressed it to himself, perhaps to a friend – just possibly to the city where he spent most of his life.

Addressed or not, Lahore today – ever in the vanguard of independent Pakistan's vigorous progress – obviously lives by just such an imperative.